365 Days of Grief Comfort

A Year of Comfort and Reflection for Moving Beyond the Loss of a Loved One or a Special Connection

Cortez Ranieri

Special Bonus

Want This _Free_ Book?

Great Free **Unlimited Access** To This Book and All My Other Books By Joining Below!

Scan W/ Your Camera

from various sources. Please consult a licensed professional before attempting any techniques outlined in this book.

By reading this document, the reader agrees that under no circumstances is the author responsible for any losses, direct or indirect, that are incurred as a result of the use of the information contained within this document, including, but not limited to, errors, omissions, or inaccuracies.

Table of Contents

Introduction

"There is no pain so great as the memory of joy in present grief," Aeschylus, the ancient Greek tragedian, once lamented.

You know first hand how right he was. Nothing is comparable to the pain you feel when you long for a lost loved one. You think about all the memories you made with them and, with each memory, it feels like you're closer and closer to breaking down.

I know how you feel. I've been there. Shocked, sad, terrified of what the future holds, desperately trying to keep their memory alive, but feeling a phantom knife twist in my gut everytime I remembered how happy I was in that moment. How happy *we* were.

There was seemingly no end to the pain I felt day in and day out. I started wondering if there was some kind of cure that I could get from a doctor or a psychiatrist; some sort of magic pill that would make everything suddenly ok again, somehow.

Of course, there was no such thing. There's no easy way out of grief from losing a loved one.

It took much trial and error, much avoidance and many painful feelings, but I ultimately managed to pull myself out of that dark abyss of despair. I haven't forgotten the people I've lost—not at all—but I'm at a place in my life where I can remember them fondly, instead of painfully.

Through my journeys and studies over the past five years, I have tried to help as many people as I can to come to terms with their loss and get through their grief. In turn, I've learned that everyone grieves differently and that not everyone's grief is like mine. So, using the knowledge I've gained from my own experience and the experiences of those I've helped, I've written this book with as many different types of people and situations in mind as I could, so that—no matter who you are and what your story is—you can benefit from something here.

I know you're probably looking for answers about how to address your own grief and come out unscathed, and you're not reading this book to hear about my life story. So let's get swiftly into the heart of it.

Part 1:

January - April

Chapter 1:
There's a Way to Grieve

The Internal Feeling of Grief

Let's begin with the single most important question: What exactly is *grief?* The Merriam Webster dictionary defines grief as "deep sadness caused especially by someone's death," and while that definition is true, it is a very basic and broad view of grief.

Grief refers to the deep, internal feelings you experience after you lose something or someone dear to you. It's intense, and can feel overwhelming and impossible to get through. Over time, however, it can slowly begin to dissipate until it's no longer crushing.

You'll feel like you can effectively move forward with your life. This entire process—from the initial intensity to the dull ache—is the grieving process.

Isn't Grief Just Another Word for Being Sad?

Well, no. Grief comes with all sorts of emotions, one of the most poignant ones being sadness, but a better way to describe it would be *distress*. It can manifest in any kind of way that one might find distressing, such as anger, fear, guilt, confusion, anxiety, insomnia, and many other symptoms. While grief is very much a psychological and emotional feeling, it can also cause physical symptoms.

So What Causes Grief?

The most common and universal cause of grief is the death of a loved one, as losing somebody in that way results in the most intense feelings of loss and is generally the hardest to overcome. However, it's not at all limited to losing someone in death, there are many other types of loss that can lead to grief. Such as:

- The loss of a relationship, or a divorce

- The loss of a job

- The loss of freedom

- The loss of stability, usually financial

- A major medical diagnosis

- A miscarriage

- The loss of a pet, whether through death, theft, or other factors

- The loss of independence due to disability

- The loss of an important item

- The loss of a future aspiration

There are no rules when it comes to what you're allowed to grieve over. If it was important to you and you've lost it in any way, you should feel the right to grieve over it. Grief is such a subjective, personal thing that sometimes it can even arise as a result of positive changes, such as leaving home, graduating from school or college, or getting a new—possibly better—job. Even non corporeal things can be mourned, such as plans that had to be canceled or dreams that have no way of being made into reality. Grief can come from many places, with many levels of severity, and it's important that you understand that, no matter what is causing you grief, that grief is equally as valid as somebody else's. Even if others see your loss as something insignificant or unimportant, if it meant something to you, you should allow yourself to grieve without casting judgment on yourself.

Please note that, although I will mainly talk about losing a loved one in this book, many of the tools and ideas are equally as effective for other types of grief as well.

The External Outlet: The Difference Between Mourning and Grieving

Mourning and *grieving* are interlocked, yet different.

While grief is a personal, internal process that each affected person has to deal with, mourning is an outward projection or action; most often performed within the first few days following the loss or on special occasions relating to the deceased.

Mourning the death of a loved one is heavily based on beliefs, customs, and religion. It's the physical, outward expression of that grief. Immediately following a person's death, a mourning ritual may begin, depending on your relation to that person, your family, your beliefs, etc. In one culture, it is customary to give flowers to the deceased's family prior to the funeral, and also to kiss the deceased's cheek at the funeral. In another culture, it's customary to give the bereaved family monetary gifts during a three day period in which they stay with the body before the funeral takes place.

Mourning may also be an ongoing or yearly thing, such as the family getting together every year on the anniversary of someone's death or, if you've lost a spouse, having a celebration of their life on your wedding anniversary.

Mourning doesn't *have* to go hand in hand with grief. Yes, if you've lost someone, you will personally go through both the internal process of grief and the external process of mourning, but even those whose lives are not as affected as yours may also go through the mourning process *with you* by attending the funeral. Those people may not be experiencing grief, at least not to the extent that you are, but they are also mourning.

Is There a Roadmap? How Can a Person Navigate Their Grief?

So where do you start? Is there a linear road that will take you to the end of your suffering? The short answer is, unfortunately, no. The long answer is that there is a *suggested* path, but it's sadly not as straightforward as you may hope.

This isn't meant to discourage you at all or make you feel like you're going to be wandering around in circles, not knowing what to do or where to turn forever. What I'm saying is that it's going to be a bumpy ride. There's going to be potholes, turns that you don't see coming, turn offs that you miss and have to circle back around to at a later time—it's going to be a perilous journey.

But you will get to a point where the road will get smoother and smoother, until the few bumps here and there won't send you spinning out of control.

Grief isn't something that can fully be explained unless you've experienced it yourself. Figuring out how to deal with it can be scary and overwhelming, and that's on top of the feelings of shock and sadness that you may be experiencing as well. People often find their own ways of coping automatically, some of which are healthy, and some not. Some throw themselves into work and stay busy to keep their minds off of it, some retreat into themselves and feel like they're safe if they don't face the outside world, some Google excessively about what they're supposed to do and how they're supposed to feel, and some simply slap a smile on their face and act like they're ok. These things, when done in excess and used as a bandaid over your wound of grief instead of simply as a coping mechanism, can be detrimental. I'll address this in more detail a little further on.

There's no one size fits all when it comes to recovery, but there are a few things that have been known to help people come to terms with their grief. Think about which of the following things will work for you and give them a try. All of these suggestions are possible offshoots of the road you're already on, so if you feel like you don't want to take that turn or you want to come back to it later, feel free to navigate the road however you wish.

Reminisce

There's a famous saying by Dr. Seuss: "Don't cry because it's over, smile because it happened."

Now, as you'll see a few lines down, I completely encourage you to cry if you feel like it, but the main message of the quote is to remember the past fondly, instead of only focusing on the negative. Reminiscing on a person's life and all the memories you have with them can be incredibly healing. You have all these memories that will stay with you forever and that's a great way to immortalize them and keep them as a part of your life. Remember that your story with your loved one isn't just about the ending, it's about everything— good, bad, happy, and sad—that you experienced before that.

Talk to Someone

For many people, talking to someone about your feelings, or even just telling somebody stories about your loved one, is the best way to heal from a loss. Often, when we face loss, we feel alone and isolated; as if we're stuck in place by ourselves while everybody else is moving forward with their lives. It may be the easiest, most natural instinct to just hide away and try to 'deal with it yourself' until you feel well enough to face the world and all the people in it again, but talking to somebody early on can help you to not feel that way in the first place.

I know it sounds scary, being open and vulnerable like that. You might think: What if I'm overreacting? The rest of my family seems fine already, I'm just being overdramatic. They wouldn't understand how I feel anyway, so what's the point? These and other similar sorts of thoughts seem to be running around in your head whenever you think of attempting to talk to someone, but I promise you that talking to someone you trust and getting it off your chest. Even if you just start with something simple: 'I'm sad'. It could make a huge difference in the burden you're carrying.

Let somebody help you carry it. Even if it's just one tiny bit of it.

Write

Like with talking to someone, writing down your feelings and thoughts can be just as healing.

It's an interesting psychological process, but writing things down has a similar mental effect as talking to someone, except instead of placing some of your burden on another person, you're placing it on paper. Think about how much more relaxed you feel once you write a shopping list instead of just going to the store and trying to remember everything while you're there. It's the same as when you write down your feelings, you're letting go of that burden instead of keeping it in your mind.

Chapter three of this book is entirely about journaling and writing things down, so we will go into more detail then. In the meantime, if you have a nice journal or even just some pieces of paper, try writing down how you're feeling.

Remember Their Favorite Things

Is there a movie that you're sure your loved one has seen about a hundred times? A playlist of songs that they would put on during every car ride? Maybe a particular book that they always recommended or a perfume that they wore for years because it was the best scent in the world to them?

It might be incredibly difficult at first to reminisce on their favorite things, perhaps even more difficult than just thinking about them; because it's something external that's influencing your memories, rather than your own, controllable thoughts. Still, getting to a point where you can listen to their favorite song with a smile on your face, thinking about all the times that particular song made them happy, is a very possible and very healthy goal. As with anything in the grieving process, start slowly, at your own pace and in your own time. For example, if they had a favorite movie, start by simply thinking about what you remember of that movie; be that a specific scene, or one or two lines, or even the song that played while the credits rolled. Once you can do that with relative ease, if you still feel like you can't watch the movie just yet, look up the poster or some screenshots online until even that is comfortable. When you finally watch the movie, you can choose to watch it with another person for support, or by yourself if you feel like that would be better.

Why is doing this even important? Think of it as a celebration. Your loved one had many likes and dislikes, many phases, many episodes of their life that made them uniquely *them*. By reflecting on their favorite things, you remember them for the person they were and that there was so much more to them than just their death.

Cry

This one seems obvious, but it can be way more beneficial than you may realize.

Without getting too much into the science of everything, crying can do a lot for your brain and, by extension, your body. Believe it or not, your brain actually releases endorphins when you cry—that's the happy chemical that helps dull physical and mental pain. You may have also noticed that you become tired after you've cried for a bit, that's because crying also soothes you, despite how counterintuitive that may sound.

Even when not grieving, many people cry when they feel angry, stressed, or even happy. It is believed that emotional crying releases toxins and the puffs of air you take in cools your brain down, which—along with relaxing you—allows you to think clearer and more rationally afterward.

So cry when you feel like crying. As long as it's not excessive (i.e. continuous or recurring), it can help a lot to calm you down and help you release some of your tension.

Talk to a Professional

When dealing with loss, grief, and all the terrible thoughts and feelings that come with it, it's highly encouraged that you speak to a therapist or a counselor. Sure, you may have a great support system and that's wonderful and super helpful, but therapists—or even more specifically, grief counselors—are trained to help you deal with exactly what you're going through. Talking to a friend may alleviate some of the burden you're carrying, but talking to a professional who can give you tailored help and advice can accelerate your healing process. I've included a few activities in this book for you to do, but if you feel like you need deeper counseling, a therapist could give you that extra push.

Of course, therapy isn't the best option for everyone. It depends heavily on you and especially on the therapist, so if you give it a try and you don't feel like it's doing you any good, don't be too hard on yourself. You're not beyond help. You won't be sad for the rest of your life. Just try a different therapist or give one of the other suggestions in this book a try.

Give Yourself Time and Space

Above everything—above talking, writing, remembering, crying, and getting professional help—

the single most important thing to do while grieving is to be nice to yourself.

I'm going to repeat that: Be nice to yourself.

Remove the word 'should' from your vocabulary when it comes to the grieving process: "By now, I *should* be able to think about them without crying. I *should* be further along in the healing process, but I feel like I'm not progressing as I *should*. Everyone's going through a hard time right now, so I *should* be strong for them."

No two people are the same, and everybody is going to move at their own pace. Comparing your journey to someone else's, or even just to how you think things *should* be going, is one of the least helpful things you can do in any situation, let alone while grieving.

Instead, you need to be patient with yourself and give yourself the time and space that is necessary for you. Think of yourself as your best friend. If you had a friend that came up to you and told you that they were going through a hard time after a major loss, chances are you wouldn't tell them to just suck it up because everybody else has moved on—or, on the other hand, that everybody else is suffering just as much as they are—so why would you talk to yourself that way? Growing up, we're all taught that we must be kind to others, but for some reason, it's so much harder to be kind to ourselves.

Practice being nice to yourself, give yourself space and try not to judge.

The Dangers of Ignoring Grief

Grief is a difficult emotion to deal with. We want to just bury it deep down inside ourselves and hope that it goes away instead of facing it head on, because that would mean exposing ourselves to all the pain, fear, and sadness that comes with it.

For some of us, trying our hardest to ignore negative feelings, and choosing to instead slap some figurative duct tape over it—hoping that it will never get out—is an automatic reaction. Some of us drown ourselves in productive things like work, family, school, or hobbies in order to keep our minds off our grief, others turn to destructive things like alcohol and drugs in a desperate attempt to just feel *ok*. Despite the fact that one is obviously worse than the other, both of those avenues are very unhealthy.

Unresolved grief is the result of not facing your pain and taking the steps to work through it. It stays with you, long after you thought you had banished it to the deepest, most isolated corner of your mind, which—in a cruel twist—actually makes the feelings that you're trying to get rid of stick around much longer than if you *hadn't* tried to ignore them.

I remember being given a little exercise to do a few years ago that I want you to try right now. You may have heard of it: It's called the Pink Elephant problem. Ready?

For ten seconds, do not—I repeat, *do not*—no matter what, think of a pink elephant. You cannot think about any pink elephants at all. Stop thinking about the pink elephant. Think about something else, don't think about any pink elephants.

Ok. So, how did that go? Chances are, you just *could not* stop thinking about that pink elephant, even though I specifically told you not to. This is called the ironic process theory, a psychological term wherein the more you try not to think about something, the more you end up thinking about it. The same is true for grieving, if you swap out the pink elephant for all the dark, scary, and depressive thoughts you may be having. You can see how futile it is to try *not* to think about something.

Ignoring grief doesn't just result in mental torment, you could also find yourself developing some physical symptoms along with it.

The following is a list of common symptoms that arise with unresolved grief:

- Anxiety

- Depression

- Insomnia

- Nightmares

- Muscle aches or tension

- Loss of appetite

- Digestion issues

And that's not even mentioning that it's a huge cause of stress and we all know that stress can have some pretty nasty effects on your physical wellbeing.

But what if you *have* to ignore it? Or at least, push it down for the time being? There's a name for that too: It's called delayed grief. Delayed grief and unresolved grief are two different things.

Say, for example, someone you love has passed away and you are one of the main people in charge of making funeral arrangements. Maybe you have family in another country and you have to liaise with them about taking a flight in order to attend. You also have to now worry about people coming in from out of state and some of them might even be staying with you for a few days, so you have to make sure the guest room is in a livable state, and that you have enough food to accommodate them and anyone else who may come over to see you. Oh, and on top of all that, your loved one had no life insurance, so you have to figure out how you're going to pay for the funeral and also somehow pay rent at the end of the month. You're busy. Extremely busy. So busy that you genuinely don't have the time to really grieve in a healthy way.

In that case, once everything slows down and you have a chance to breathe again, *then* the grieving process can begin. That's why it's called delayed grief. You're not trying to ignore it, you just have a million other things that you have to get done before you can really take the time to acknowledge it and give it the attention it needs.

Unresolved grief—the unhealthy kind—comes from a conscious decision to ignore your grief and pretend that everything is ok, or at least that *you're* ok.

On a side note, some people may experience a different type of delayed grief: where you feel like you're ok and then a few weeks or months down the line, everything hits you at once. This is also normal, and you can rest assured that, as long as you go through your grieving journey—no matter when that journey may begin—you will not have to experience unresolved grief and all the effects that come with it.

Why 365 Days? Why not a Month or a Few Weeks?

Some people might think that grieving is what you do in the days following the loss of a loved one, but that's only partly true. Grieving can happen for many reasons, as I will explain in the next section, and it can last anywhere from just a few months to years. Grieving is a very personal thing. Everyone grieves differently and everyone takes a different amount of time to heal. Someone might feel like their life is pretty much back to normal after a few months while others may need years to get adjusted. Grief isn't something you can snap your fingers and get over, there are processes and steps—

both automatic and deliberate—that one must take to overcome it.

So why do we say 365 days? Well, one year is generally enough time to figure out what works for you and to already be on your road to healing. It's not set in stone that you *will* experience the things discussed in this book in specific months of the year, obviously, so if you feel like you're already at the point of chapter three while it's only been one or two months since your loss, there's nothing stopping you from skipping ahead or even reading completely out of order. Try not to take the months as a hard and fast rule, simply use it as guidance.

That being said, most often, grieving takes time. Losing something or someone that was important in your life isn't just something you can heal from overnight. Things have changed in your life and you need to give yourself time to come to terms with that.

It's also important to note that "getting over" your grief doesn't mean that, after the grieving process, you'll be 100% back to normal and everything will be ok. What it does mean is that you'll be better equipped to go through life with a new sense of normalcy, and hopefully, not wallow in sadness. Sometimes you may not even feel like you're progressing. Sometimes you might feel like you've taken one step forward and two steps back, or that you're not 'keeping up' with the timeline. I can't stress this enough: Everyone heals at their own pace. You may hear me say that a few more times in this book, but it's crucial to your healing process that you give yourself the time that you personally need and not be too concerned about where you think you *should* be in the journey.

Remember: Being kind to yourself is the most important part of grieving.

Worksheet #1

Grief Response

Take note of what feelings and emotions you've experienced since the loss of your loved one.

- Anxiety
- Trouble Sleeping
- Irritability
- Numbness

- Sadness
- Crying
- Guilt
- Confusion

Which of those are causing you the most distress at the moment?

_____
_____.

Elaborate a little (when do you experience it, how bad is it, etc.).

_____
_____.

What is causing that feeling/emotion/or problem?

_____
_____.

What can you do right now to feel a little better?

_____
_____.

What can you do tomorrow that will help you heal?

_____
_____.

Chapter 2:

One Day at a Time

How to Take It One Day at a Time

I want you to think back to when you were a child. If you were anything like me, your room was messy all the time and your mother constantly nagged at you to clean it. You, yourself wanted a clean room too, you just didn't want to actually do the whole cleaning part. It felt like such a huge job and you couldn't see how you could *possibly* get all of the clothes, books, toys, or whatever else was causing the clutter, to be neat and tidy. What I used to do back then was stand in my doorway (or on my bed) and survey the room. Then I would take a piece of paper and write down everything I had to do in order to make it clean, and then organize it in a to-do list, bullet point style, in order of easiest to hardest, or what would only be possible to do after first completing something else, like vacuuming. Then I would get to work. I would most likely get distracted at some point and most of the time, I couldn't finish it in one day because of said distractions (or just because I got lazy), but at some point, everything on that list would eventually be ticked off and my room would be clean.

You might be wondering why I'm telling you about what a messy child I was. I'm not here to teach you about cleaning techniques, after all.

The reason I started this chapter with that analogy is to give you a practical—and mostly universal—idea of how something can seem like a huge, imposing mountain in front of you, way too big to tackle. You may have a 20,000 word college dissertation or you may have a huge pile of paperwork that makes you want to curl up when you even just think about it. However, by breaking those tasks down and focusing on one thing at a time, it makes the whole project seem more doable and, if you keep at it, you will get it done.

That's the point: Focus only on one thing at a time. In terms of the grieving process, focus only on one day at a time.

If you focus too much on the goal of "getting over it" and you don't see instant results, it's easy to think that you're never going to be happy again and that you don't know how you're going to be able to live after this. It's hard, but the only way to get through it is to take it one day at a time.

So, what does that mean?

The first thing you need to do is get out of bed in the morning. Congratulations! You've already ticked off your first bullet point! If you managed to brush your teeth and take a shower, then that's two more boxes done. Made your bed? That's another.

From there, it all depends on your current emotional state and your lifestyle. If you're not back at work yet (or you don't work), then try doing at least one productive task a day, like cooking a nice meal or engaging in a hobby. Staying focused on the present and the things that you're doing right now, instead of what may seem like an endless journey ahead will help keep you grounded and stop you from feeling overwhelmed.

Of course, some days, it will be easier to do these tasks than others, and that's ok. If one day you feel that you really cannot do anything productive and you even have to force yourself into the bathroom to brush your teeth, that's perfectly fine and perfectly normal. Just try again tomorrow.

Here are a few more suggestions on how to get through the day:

Talk

I've mentioned how important it is to talk to someone you trust about how you feel, but it's equally important to talk to someone about simple, mundane, everyday things too. You saw a pretty bird land on your windowsill this morning. Your dog did something really cute and you just missed getting it on video.

Talk to a family member or friend about what you both had for lunch that day; was it good? Did you eat something for the first time in a long time? Did the fast food place put onions in your burger even though you asked them not to? Or maybe the turkey sandwich you had was particularly delicious today because you used a new sauce that you bought recently. Conversation, no matter how mundane, is one of the most healing things you can do when going through grief. I keep emphasizing this, but there is a good reason for that. I promise, it will make you feel just a little lighter, even if it's only for those few minutes that you're actually talking, it's still an escape from your grief.

Schedule

This fits in with what I spoke about earlier. The best way to get through a day is to have a schedule, otherwise you may end up feeling overwhelmed and all over the place, not knowing what to do or where to start. Scheduling your day, even if it's just roughly like in a to-do format instead of time based, can give you the structure you need to get through it effectively.

Having a schedule doesn't mean packing it either. Make sure you have some breathing room, in case something doesn't go as planned. Maybe you underestimated how long a specific task would take, or something else came up. The goal is simply to not wallow in grief or stay inside your own head the whole day, not to make yourself so busy that you start to ignore the grief entirely.

Get Some Fresh Air and Sunshine

The sun is a natural antidepressant and getting out of the house from time to time may be just what you need in order to calm yourself down and get your mind back to a healthier place. Preferably, try not to go out by yourself, rather go with a friend or family member. Firstly, because having some company is always good when you're grieving, and secondly because you may encounter all sorts of grief triggers out in the world and having someone who understands what you're going through to fall back on is a good idea, so you won't have to face those triggers alne.

Go for brunch with a friend, go for a walk together, or even go for a gym date together. Whatever you feel will help you in the moment.

Pamper Yourself

When you're feeling terrible, the last thing you want to do is something that seems superficial or even selfish, but getting a relaxing massage or a refreshing facial can be just the thing you need. Why not book a spa day with a friend or a sibling and just spend the day drinking champagne and getting tended to?

Another option is to treat yourself to a fancy dinner. Go to that restaurant that you always wanted to and order that lobster you've always wanted to try. If spending that much money is just making you more anxious, then why not go to that cute, cozy little coffee shop you passed before, and have a cappuccino and a slice of cheesecake?

If possible, getting away for a weekend may also be healing. You don't even need to book a fancy hotel in Hawaii or anything like that, you can always just find a resort near you that's within driving distance of home, just in case you decide you don't want to stay there. Or you could ask someone close to you if you could spend a night at their place. A change of scenery is good to help you reset and relieve some of that stress.

Stay Distracted

If you live alone or are by yourself for a good part of the day, you know that sometimes the silence can be deafening, and that is amplified by a thousand when you're going through emotional turmoil. Sometimes just turning the tv on and letting whatever infomercial is on at that time play in the background while you go through your day is enough to fill that overwhelming silence.

If you prefer keeping your mind on something instead of just having background noise, listening to music, an interesting podcast, an audiobook or a YouTube video of something that interests you may be a better idea. I feel like it's pretty obvious, but filling that silence with something depressing or dark is perhaps not the best idea (but hey, if it helps you relax and get through the day, then to each their own).

Schedule Your Grief

Grief is unpredictable. One minute you might be ok, ready to face whatever comes your way, and then you feel like you're on the edge of a breakdown. It's not uncommon to have the sudden urge to run away and curl into a ball when you're out with friends and a song reminds you of the person, or when you're at work and you see someone who has the same name as your loved one. There is an effective method of dealing with this though: we refer to it as "scheduling your grief". This is a commonly used method for those who suffer with anxiety, but it's equally effective for those going through grief as well.

All you need to do is, when a painful thought, memory, or feeling comes up, don't attempt to ignore it—don't think about the pink elephant, remember?—instead, acknowledge that it's there and tell it, and yourself, that you will address it later. At a more opportune time, like when you get home, after you take a shower, or once you're just a little more relaxed. The biggest part of this technique though, is that you actually stick to your schedule and give yourself a few minutes to think about the painful thought. If you don't go through with it, you won't be able to trick your mind into giving you peace when you need it.

Laugh

Laughing is one of the hardest things to do when you're grieving. You can fake a smile, but genuine laughter doesn't come easily. Despite it being one of the most *difficult* things, it's also one of the *best* things to help you heal. There's a reason laughing yoga exists. If you're unaware, laughing yoga is where a group of people get together regularly to laugh. It sounds funny, and it is funny when you see a bunch of people in a circle laughing like crows, but that's the point, it's supposed to be funny. You force a laugh, you realize how ridiculous you and everyone around you sounds, and then you end up laughing for real. Try it, it's surprisingly liberating. Even if you think it's a really weird thing to do, try it when you're home alone or with a friend or family member. I promise you, it will be so weird that you won't be able to help but laugh.

On a bit of a more serious note, sometimes after a loss, we may feel like we *shouldn't* laugh. This is not true. Laughing during a funeral is not always the best thing to do, but the days following should not have to be as somber. Allow yourself to laugh. Laughter is the best medicine, after all.

Dealing with Other Divorce Grief

As I mentioned earlier, grief isn't always a result of the death of a loved one. You can grieve for someone who is still very much alive, but is lost to *you* for some reason or the other. One of the hardest forms of grief come from the loss of a relationship, be it a marriage or a long term romance.

Yes, when you get divorced or break up with a long term partner, it's not just sadness that you go through; it's grief. Depending on how long the relationship lasted and how messy it ended, the grief you feel from a loss of a relationship can be comparable to losing someone in death. Some argue that it can be even worse, stating that you have no choice but to accept loss when someone close to you passes away, but when you lose a partner, you have to live with the fact that they're still out there, but they're forever out of your reach. A person's death also isn't often the result of something that you personally did, while a divorce or break up can be and, depending on the circumstances, you may feel extreme guilt over the situation.

So don't feel like you're being dramatic if the loss of a relationship devastates you.

Whatever caused the relationship to decline can play a major role in how bad the grief you feel afterwards is. One of the major causes of a divorce or breakup is infidelity. If you were the guilty party, you're most likely going to feel a huge amount of guilt over the entire situation. However, you can also experience guilt if you were the one being cheated on, because sometimes our brains trick us into thinking that we did something to warrant our partner going out and finding someone else in the first place. No matter what is causing you guilt, you have to understand that what happened has already happened. If you've tried to mend the relationship in the past and failed to do so, then the only thing you can do is accept it and focus on the *here* and *now,* instead of wishing that you'd done something different. I know that sounds easier said than done—and it definitely is—but if you just keep taking things one day at a time, everything will come together.

In addition to some of the other suggestions mentioned earlier, here are a few extra things that pertain specifically to this type of grief that you can try out.

Talk to Someone

Yes, this was in the previous part, but it's a little different when you're going through the loss of a relationship. When somebody passes away, their death is likely to affect a wide variety of people on many different levels, so there's a sense of camaraderie among people who were close to the deceased. With the breakdown of a relationship, nobody else is going to feel the effects as much as you and your ex partner will, so you may feel far more isolated and unsure of how to approach somebody to begin talking to them about everything. Unless they've been in a similar situation before, your friends and family are not going to understand how you feel, but that's ok, you don't need them to. Simply ranting to someone you trust, whether it's in anger or sadness, or just having a shoulder to cry on can be a huge step forward in the grieving process. Try not to aim to be understood, just aim to be heard.

Don't Hide From Your Children

If you have children with your ex partner, it's easy to try and shield them from everything by putting on a façade because you think you have to be strong for them. In a way, that is true—you don't want to put your burden on your kids' shoulders—but that doesn't mean you can't tell them that you're also affected by everything that's happening. Now, that's not to say you should bawl your eyes out and curse your ex angrily in front of your kids—don't do this—but letting them know that you're also sad is healing in two avenues:

- For you, because you can let a little piece of that strong mask go, and you're allowed to be upset, even when your kids are around.

- For your kids, because children mimic their parents, and if they see that you're opening up and allowing yourself to be emotionally vulnerable, they themselves will find it a little easier to open up to you.

So let your kids know that it's ok and perfectly normal to be upset about things like this, but just try not to let them in on the grittier side. Use your discretion and take their ages into consideration.

Let Go

No matter what caused the end of the relationship, you're likely to feel some anger towards the other party at some point, this is especially true if it ended in a messy way. This anger may even be justified if you were wronged in some way, so don't feel like a bad person for being angry. However, holding on to that anger is going to do you more harm than good. Holding grudges is terrible for both your mental and physical health and can affect you long term because of the high amounts of stress that you're unwittingly putting yourself through.

Forgiveness might be incredibly difficult, and hell, if there's nothing connecting the two of you anymore—if you don't share a child, for example—then you don't have to forgive them at all. But you have to let go of the anger; it's not going to do anything for you aside from making you sick.

Wait

When we're suddenly thrust into this world where we don't have a partner at our side and are forced to go it alone, we can often start looking for a replacement way too soon. It's not a good idea to get into a relationship right away, your focus should be on getting over the one that just ended first. If you start dating right away, you may find yourself in a situation where your new partner begins to feel like they're just a rebound or you might wrongly convince yourself that you love this person, when really you're just trying to fill the void left by your ex partner. Give yourself time to grieve the lost relationship first before jumping head first into another one.

Check in on Yourself

Grief lasts a long time, so expecting yourself to be A-ok in a week is not practical. But every now and then, check in with yourself to see if you're actually healing in a healthy way. If a few months down the line, you feel like you've made no progress or your grief just keeps getting worse and worse over time, then you should consider contacting a professional. Grief from a divorce can easily turn into depression in the long run, so don't be ashamed to ask for professional help if you feel like you're going down that road.

Grieving Someone with Whom You Cut Ties

There are countless reasons why you may have had to cut ties with a person previously close to you. Whether that's a parent, a child, a friend, a family member or a lover; often, being around specific people who have hurt you deeply is not the best thing for you.

Consider: If your partner who you've loved for years has become abusive to you recently—whether that's mentally, physically, or emotionally—you need to seriously consider cutting them out of your life, for your own health and well-being. That might seem obvious, 'This person is detrimental to me and my life, I have to let them go', and yes, you should, but it may not be as easy as it sounds.

Loss of a person, no matter how positive that loss may be, can cause you a lot of grief and heartache.

This kind of grief can be incredibly confusing. On the one hand, you feel relief, and your mind logically understands that this separation is for the best. But on the other hand, you still feel like you lost someone close to you. You feel like you *shouldn't* be upset and you may even keep telling yourself that, but you're a hundred percent justified in your feelings. You may even try to convince yourself that what you're feeling can't be grief; why would you grieve over someone who made you miserable? So whether you're cutting ties with a narcissistic parent, a rebellious child, or anyone else that has caused you pain, you are allowed to grieve.

When it comes to cutting people out of your life, as I mentioned, things can get a lot more complicated than when you're grieving for someone who passed away. You might still be holding onto a futile hope, no matter how unlikely it seems, that you can somehow repair the relationship and everything will be better. No matter the reason that caused you to ultimately decide to remove this person from your life, you likely loved them a lot in the years preceding it, so naturally, you will feel grief over no longer having them around.

Even if the relationship was tumultuous for a long time, consider: You may not be grieving the loss of that person, but the loss of the relationship that you wished you had with them. Try and look at it from an objective point of view: Are you sad that they're gone, or are you sad that you won't have a chance to *maybe* have a good relationship with them?

So how can you overcome this? Well, many of the techniques mentioned in the loss of a relationship section are relevant for cutting toxic people out of your life, too. Namely: Letting go, checking in on yourself, and talking to someone.

One thing that may be a bit more complicated in this case, especially if the person you're cutting out of your life is a family member, is that other people close to you might feel differently about that person than you do. You'll have to find a nice balance when figuring out who to talk to about your feelings and frustrations: Who to be more civil around, who you can trust, and who to avoid entirely when talking about *that* person you've cut from your life. This can take some trial and error, unfortunately, as we don't usually know how somebody feels until we've unwillingly offended them. Try to get a clear sense of how a person feels about the one you've cut out before dumping all your frustrations on them.

I will talk more about journaling in the next chapter, but writing things down may also be helpful in this case, if you don't want to step on anyone's toes. Some people also find it cathartic to write a letter directed to the person who hurt them, and then get rid of it by burning it or something of the like; perhaps to symbolize letting go.

Just remember: Cutting someone out because they're making life unbearable doesn't make you a bad person, no matter what anyone else says.

Worksheet #2

Non-Death Grief

Fill in the following prompts (if your grief is about a loved one, you can still fill in the worksheet):

My grief is about

_____

_____.

How is it causing changes in your life at the moment?

_____

_____.

It hurts because

_____

_____

_____.

Today has been (easier than/harder than/the same as) yesterday.

My biggest worry is

_____
_____.

My hope for the future is

_____
_____
_____.

What would have to happen for that hope to become a reality?

_____
_____
_____.

What is the next step I have to take?

_____
_____.

Chapter 3:

Journaling Through

The Simple Power of Journaling Through

Ah, journaling. It's one of the most effective, most cathartic things you can do to calm your mind and heal your soul. It has been proven again and again, over many years, that journaling is an effective way to manage stress and anxiety. It also can help you learn things about yourself that you may not have noticed during the busier days you experienced throughout your life.

But you might ask: What makes journaling so good, and so appealing to so many people?

Easy to Do

You may disagree with me on this. If you look up journals online, you'll see all kinds of pretty, perfectly laid out daily spreads. They're filled with colors, pictures, drawings, and stickers, and you'll probably think to yourself that you don't have the time or the creativity for that. That's fine. Those perfect journals that are somewhere between a journal, planner, and a scrapbook? That's not what we're looking for.

A journal is just a place for you to write your thoughts and feelings. Nobody is going to see it, so stressing about making it perfect is a non-issue. All you need is a pen and paper (or an electronic device) and you can begin journaling immediately.

Private

During the grieving process, especially in the early stages, you may feel apprehensive about talking to another person. This could be because you don't actually know how to put your feelings into words, or you just don't feel like it, or many other reasons. In that case, journaling is great because you still get things off your chest without the fear of being judged or coming across as incoherent. In certain complicated situations, you may also not have anyone close to you that you *can* talk to, but it is crucial not to bottle your feelings up. Journaling could be the best way to let them out.

Grounding

Sometimes—especially when you're going through grief—your thoughts can get all jumbled up inside your head, and you may have a hard time pinning them down before more messy thoughts flood in and take their place. When you write things down, you're forced to *slow* down and really think about the way you're feeling and the thoughts you're having. In turn, they become more solid, and you can look at them with more clarity and objectivity than if it was one of the many thoughts passing through your mind. In this way, you also ultimately become more aware of your thoughts and emotions during the rest of the day, because you can now mentally put certain feelings into words immediately like you did on paper.

Journaling also forces you to be a friend to yourself. You rant to your journal as if you were ranting to a friend, but then you also have to allow yourself to mentally reply the way you would to a friend too. It's always harder to be nice to ourselves than other people, but distancing yourself from your own words and then replying gently to them as if you were comforting a friend can help.

Counteracts Avoidance

Avoidance is one of the worst things those who are grieving can do. Avoidance leads to unresolved grief (see chapter 1), which is terrible for you on so many levels. Unfortunately for a lot of people, avoidance is also the easiest thing to do, especially when your days are busy and you don't have much time to feel your grief. Just the simple act of writing down a bit of how you feel can contribute to healing and keep you from falling into the trap of avoidance.

Flexible

If you want to make journaling an everyday habit (which, if you're in the early stages of grief, I encourage you to do), it's going to take some level of discipline and consistency, until it becomes a habit. However, journaling daily doesn't necessarily mean that you have to take 30 minutes every night to write out your thoughts before you go to bed. You can journal whenever, wherever, and however you want.

Do you prefer to write first thing in the morning? Write first thing in the morning. Do you get stressed around lunch time? Take your journal to work and write during your break. Do your bouts of wanting to write come up randomly day to day? No problem. Keep your journal with you (or simply grab your phone) and write whenever the mood strikes you. There are no rules. It's about you.

If you don't want to journal every single day, you definitely don't have to. You can choose to do it whenever you feel like it. Weekly, only on the weekends, or whenever you need to, these are all ok.

Impacts Physical and Mental Health

The impact that journaling has on mental health is very visible and sometimes instantaneous. For some, its effects on things like anxiety and depression are even comparable to taking medication; but did you know that it can also positively affect your physical health?

I've talked about stress before and how it can wreak havoc on your body, journaling—or throwing all your worries, anxieties, and stress onto the book instead of keeping it in—can help you manage stress, or even help you to let go of whatever is causing you stress in the first place. Objectively looking at something can help you see it in a different light and you may come to realize that, among all the real stressors in your life, you might also be letting yourself get stressed over things that don't deserve your attention in the first place. If you're going through the grieving process but you're also worried about whether or not you have the adequate amount of food or snacks in your house—should someone decide to stop by—writing all of it down will help you re-evaluate what's really important and what you can mentally let go of.

Another physical benefit of journaling is getting a good night's rest. This too goes back to stress management. When your stress levels are low, your quality of sleep improves. If you journal before you sleep and put *all* of the day's stress onto paper and leave it there, where it belongs, you can have a better night's rest.

How to Use a Journal to Heal

So now that you have an idea of how journaling helps you, you might still be a little confused about how to get started and what exactly you're supposed to do to reap the benefits (I'm going to give you a little spoiler here: the only thing you're *supposed* to do is write). There are some tips and ideas that I'd like to let you know, along with the many possible ways that you can utilize this amazing tool.

The idea of a journal (especially a grief journal) is to put your thoughts down on paper, unfiltered, unedited, and without any sugar coating so that you can get a firmer grasp on your feelings and emotions. The best way to do this is to just write anything and everything that comes into your mind. You can go on seemingly unrelated tangents, it doesn't have to be spelled perfectly, the grammar doesn't have to be perfect, it doesn't have to be complete thoughts—hell, it doesn't even have to be coherent. Even if there's not an ounce of structure, you're still fulfilling the one requirement of journaling: writing. Your journal isn't for anybody else to read, understand, or judge; so as long as it makes sense to you, that's all that matters.

If you find the thought of journaling to be rather intimidating at first, that's completely reasonable. After all, you have to let your meticulously perfected guard down and open yourself up to being vulnerable. Just the idea of having to face your thoughts can be terrifying at times. If you're not yet a hundred percent on board with opening up like that or you find it a bit weird in some way, then try starting with regular, mundane things. Write about what you did that day and what you want to do tomorrow. Your first few entries might sound super formal and thought out, but that's ok, all you need to do is get the ball rolling until you feel comfortable enough to dig deeper. There's no pressure with journaling. You move at a pace that's comfortable for you.

You should aim to be completely honest eventually. Keep reminding yourself that nobody is going to see what you wrote, so you don't have to be afraid of judgment. Write honestly, openly, and especially try *not* to avoid the particularly scary thoughts and feelings that you may be having. Those are the ones that can give you the biggest insight into yourself, as well as the biggest sense of relief to get off your chest.

There are also different ways of journaling. Some people like writing full sentences and ranting to their journal as if they were speaking to another person, while others prefer writing down only the major keywords or doing it in a bullet point form. For example, one person's entry might look something like: *"Today was quite a good day for me because I went to eat with my family. It's been a long time since we got to hang out like that, so I enjoyed myself."* While another person's entry might look something like *"Good day. Ate with family. Happier than yesterday."* Once again, this is up to personal preference, and you can even mix styles if you wish to. There is no right or wrong way to journal.

How much you write each day is also completely up to you. Whether you write one paragraph or five pages, it all just depends on your style of writing and how much you have to say on that particular day. Personally, I would recommend getting a journal that doesn't have the date at the top of every page, and rather opt for something either lined or completely blank as that will allow you to control the amount of content without being confined to one page or feeling like you're forced to pad your writing to fit the whole page.

On the subject of the types of journals, there are many different kinds out there, three of the most common being:

- **Lined Journals**: These are like notebooks that are already pre-lined and are the most common choice for someone wanting to start a journal, as you'll likely only be writing in it.

- **Blank Journals**: The pages in blank journals are just that: blank. Completely blank. This allows you to not only write your thoughts and feelings, but gives you space for any artistic expression you may want to do. If you're artsy and feel like having space to just draw or doodle your thoughts along with writing, pick up one of these blank journals.

- **Dotted Journals**: These journals contain little dots spaced out evenly throughout the pages and are a nice middle ground between lined and blank journals. The dots are placed at the same height and width apart, so you can keep your words straight without needing actual lines (of course, you can always draw a horizontal line through the dots to create lines of your own) and the dots help you with proportions and guides if you decide to draw as well.

That's just a guide of how these journals are *usually* used, but if you want to draw beautiful pictures over lined paper, there's absolutely nothing wrong with that.

There's also always the option to forgo a physical journal altogether. These days, most of us carry around phones or tablets everywhere we go, and it's become far more convenient to reach for your phone when you want to write something down instead of looking for a pen and paper. Add the fact that there are countless apps made specifically for journaling, and you may just decide to go the digital route instead. Some do argue that writing things down by hand is better for you than typing it out using predictive text or autocorrect because relying on those things takes away from the experience, but it really is a person to person thing, ultimately. If using a phone or a tablet is more comfortable for you and you feel like you're more likely to stay consistent that way, then go for it.

An important part of journaling that can so easily be overlooked is the review part. This is especially necessary when dealing with grief. Going back after some time to look at what you wrote is going to be both difficult and cathartic at the same time. In a way, you will revisit all your thoughts and emotions from back when things were at their worst, but far more objectively. You'll then be able to assess where you are now versus what your mental state was like back then, and plan your next steps from there (remember, if you feel like you've gotten worse, or you've been stuck in that horrific place for too long, don't be afraid to contact a professional).

There's also no right or wrong time to start a journal. Don't think that it won't work for you because you've already been grieving for a few months. It doesn't matter, journaling is likely to still provide some benefits for you. Alternatively, in the case of divorce, terminal illness, or anything where you can see the path that you or your loved one is walking is not going to have a happy ending; you can start journaling as early in the process as you wish to, before the worst inevitably happens.

How to Journal When You Don't Feel Like It

Have you ever tried to develop a habit? I think most of us have made a promise to ourselves that we were going to work out every single day because we want to be fit and healthy. However, there's always those days where we just don't feel like it at all. Maybe we were super busy or we felt a little under the weather, or maybe nothing was wrong, but the thought of going to the gym just made us recoil for reasons unknown to us. If you were in that situation, what would you do? You really want to stay on your fitness journey, but you feel like you may just throw a tantrum if you were to step outside of your house right now. What could you do in a situation like that?

1. Skip the workout altogether. Instead, come up with a realistic plan about how you're going to get it done tomorrow, even if you still don't feel like it. A game plan, if you will.

2. Do a little bit of light exercise around your house instead. Something like playing with your kids or the dogs out in the yard, or following one of the countless at home workout routines that you can find online, or even just doing a few jumping jacks in your living room.

There is no correct answer, they're both correct. You're allowed to not be perfect when it comes to building habits, so if you decided to just skip the workout for today and instead promise yourself that you'll definitely get back into it tomorrow; that's not going to derail all the progress you may have made before that. Sometimes we need a break from trying to be perfect. On the other hand, even just doing a little bit of something, even if it's not to the extent that you usually would, keeps that ball rolling and you can still be proud of yourself for those little victories. And who knows, maybe something as small as dancing while you do the dishes will give you the boost you need to jog around the block.

You may have guessed by now that that is an analogy for journaling (I do love my analogies). We're trying to make it a habit, but sometimes it can really feel like a chore. Whether we don't have time to write, we're tired, or we don't have anything really profound to say, there will be days where we just don't feel like writing in the journal. Like the analogy about exercising, we have two preferable courses of action to take when that happens: we can either choose not to write at all today and make a mental note to do it tomorrow instead, or we can open the journal, write one line or one tiny paragraph and close it. Any small amount of repetition helps form habits; even just jotting down a quick thought and putting it in your pocket for later, or sending yourself a text. No choice is inherently better than the other, so do whatever works best for you.

Here are some more tips for journaling when you don't feel like it.

Use Prompts

Prompts are not only great for giving yourself a little push, they're also great when you're just starting out and you don't know where to start. Have a list of relevant prompts on hand so that you won't be stuck on what to actually write. Here are a few examples of grief related prompts, but feel free to make a few of your own that you think will be beneficial to you:

- Today I feel/felt…

- Today I miss…

- I am grateful for...

- One of my favorite memories of my loved one is...

- Tomorrow will be easier if I...

- Whenever things get tough again, I will...

- What are some ways you can celebrate them?

- What's a funny memory you have of them?

- What song makes you think of them?

There's countless other prompts that might fit you better. You can even buy journals that have prompts like these already printed inside them, and you just have to take it from there if you're more comfortable with that.

Doodle

If you're the type that can express yourself through art, then just doodling in your journal can be a great way to keep up the habit without the stress of having to write something down. Even if you're not artistically expressive, just aimlessly doodling while you think about things is another good way to address your thoughts and feelings, even if you're not putting them into words. This is actually similar to doing a mindfulness exercise, which we will discuss a bit later.

Make a List

Any kind of list. What are some of your loved ones favorite songs? What were those songs that they just couldn't stand? What are some random facts about them? Even though you're not writing anything about yourself, you're still writing. The lists don't even have to be about your loved one, you could write your to do list for tomorrow or a list of *your* favorite songs. Which brings me to the last point:

Write Anything

Even though, at its core, you're keeping a grief journal, not every single entry has to have something to do with your loved one or about your feelings. You can write about literally anything you want. Once in a while, you can even take a break from writing about your life at all. If you want to write about that drama you've been watching and how Character A is so stupid for not noticing that Character B is in love with them, or about how you would have written the script differently so that they would kiss in the rain, then by all means.

Overall, journaling is a very personal, very subjective experience. If it's not for you, then it's not for you... but why not give it a try? It may end up working wonders.

Worksheet #3

Journaling

Write about your day, your feelings, or anything else. Try not to edit too much, just let your mind run wild and write.

_____

_____

_____

_____

_____

_____

_____

_____

Part 2:

May - August

Chapter 4:

Dealing with Guilt

Guilt About Being Responsible

When you think about the popular concept of the five stages of grief—shock/denial, anger, bargaining, depression, and acceptance—it seems so straightforward, as if those are the only things you should expect to go through. To some degree, it is the most common path of grief. But as you already know, nothing about going through grief is ever so predictable. One of the most common (and yet least spoken about) feelings that you may experience during grief, is guilt. There are different types of guilt, so let's start with the most common one first: Feeling as though you could have done something differently, or even done something to prevent the death.

There are two types of guilt in this case:

- Guilt over something you did.

- Guilt over something you *didn't* do.

The most common of these two is the latter; guilt over something that you didn't do.

What does that mean? Well, say, for example: Your grandmother passed away suddenly. You may immediately think about how a few months ago she asked you to come stay over at her house, and you turned down the invitation because you already had other plans. Your mind then manages to trick you into thinking that if you had gone to see her then, things somehow would have turned out differently. It's not really logical—as your presence more than likely would not have made any difference—but your mind is rarely logical when it's going through grief.

Or maybe you had a friend that needed a bone marrow transplant, but you were not compatible, and they ended up passing away while they were still on the waiting list. You had no control over that, you were just incompatible. It wasn't anything that you did or didn't do, you just *couldn't*. And yet, you still have that little voice in the back of your head saying, "If only I was a match, then they would still be alive."

You may not even know what you're feeling guilty about. You wrack your brain and come up with all sorts of impossible scenarios about how something you did or said could have saved someone, even though it doesn't make any sense. We do this because, when a tragedy happens, we automatically want to blame someone or something for it—and who's the easiest person in the world to blame? Ourselves.

This kind of guilt is irrational, but that doesn't make it any less real and, by extension, any less important.

Feeling guilt while you're grieving is far more common than people let on. They often hide it because they know that it's irrational, and yet it still eats away at them. That desire to keep it inside is only exacerbated when everyone they open up to says things like, "You have no reason to feel guilty" or "It's not your fault." Which, more often than we realize, comes from good intentions and a desire to comfort you, but may have the opposite effect. It might cause you to retreat more into yourself because you don't think that anyone else understands how you're feeling.

One of the biggest things you can do to overcome guilt is to accept it. Now, that doesn't mean that you have to accept the wrongly perceived fact that you are guilty, and that also doesn't mean that you have to accept that you're just going to feel guilty for the rest of your life. Instead, you have to accept that those feelings of guilt are going to stick around for a little while. They might be irrational, but trying to ignore them is detrimental because your mind can't see them for how irrational they are, not just yet. Remember the pink elephant? The more you try to push something down, the more it likes to worm it's way back into your mind.

Another thing is to realize how common guilt is during the grieving process, and recognize that you're not weird for feeling it.

Of course, as you may have noticed, I'm the biggest advocate for journaling or writing things down in general. So if you're feeling irrational guilt or regret about something, write it down either in a book or on a piece of paper, and then also write down what you think you should have done and what the outcome would have been, then take a—literal or figurative—step back and try to look at what you've written more objectively. Usually, doing this exercise helps you to see for yourself how irrational your guilty thoughts may be and, in turn, help you come to terms with them. You can also choose to destroy the paper afterwards as symbolism for letting it go.

Even if you don't write everything down, simply sitting in silence for a few minutes and mentally putting the same thoughts in their place (what could I have done, and what would the outcome be?) may also be beneficial in having you come to terms with everything. You could also talk to somebody you trust. You just have to make sure, in this case, that they're not going to simply tell you that it's not your fault and just expect you to accept that.

Try to turn the negative into a positive. Let your current guilt and regret mold you into a better person. What I mean by that is, say you lost your grandmother and you regret not spending much time with her during the last few years of her life. Now you can make it a point from this moment on to regularly keep in touch with your grandfather, call him regularly, go visit him, take him out for lunch sometimes—try your best to make sure that, no matter what happens in the future, you won't have the same regrets that you did when your grandmother passed away. Of course, this isn't the only way you can use guilt to make yourself better; everyone's different, depending on their circumstances. So try it today: Think about one thing you regret and how you can avoid having that regret in the future, and then think about ways to act on that.

Accepting that something was out of our control is difficult, but what if you were—either directly or indirectly—responsible for the death of your loved one? Perhaps they died in a car crash, you were the one driving the car, and maybe you knew you were overly tired and probably shouldn't have been behind the wheel that day. Or perhaps, you got so stressed and frustrated with a suicidal person who seemed to never want to get better, that you said something that may have been insensitive and served as a catalyst for them taking their own lives. Guilt over something that you did is extremely hard to get through.

The single most important thing to do in this situation is forgive yourself. That's easier said than done. Chances are, you didn't intend for the person to die—

we, as humans (in general) never want to see or hear of *anybody* dying, let alone somebody close to us—and whatever happened was just a terrible outcome to something that you did or said. I know it's hard right now, and I don't want to sound harsh at all, but you have to realize that what happened has already happened and that you can't change the past, no matter how badly you may want to. We can't predict the future, you're not a terrible person, you do deserve to move past this guilt.

Applying the techniques mentioned above may also provide some relief, but the most important thing—by *far*—is forgiveness. This isn't going to be easy. I say this for everything, but that's because it's important: If you feel like you aren't getting better or you feel like the guilt is just too overwhelming to handle, please consider seeking professional help.

Survivor's Guilt

Survivor's guilt is a terrible condition caused by trauma and is often compared to post-traumatic stress disorder (PTSD). It is most often caused by someone surviving some sort of life threatening situation in which others have died. This can be anything from a car accident, to a natural disaster, or even a pandemic. It's also alarmingly common among those who have survived serious illnesses: You can often form bonds with other people going through the same thing as you, who end up not making it. In some cases, you might feel like if *you* hadn't gotten the life-saving treatment, the other person may have survived; whether it's because there's a limited amount of treatment available (such as things like organ transplants) or through a belief such as God had to take one of you and if you hadn't survived, the other person would have.

Whether it's small scale or something huge, whether one person died or a hundred did, if you survive something that very easily could have killed you too, you could be forced to deal with survivor's guilt. Thankfully, not everybody in these situations struggle with survivor's guilt. It has instead been shown to develop more often in people with a history of depression, or even among children. Of course, just because it isn't as common as other parts of grief, doesn't mean it's not as important.

"You're Alive, You Should be Happy/Thankful/Grateful"

If you've ever told anyone about your guilt over surviving a traumatic event, you may have heard something like that being said to you. They mean it in the best way; they're just trying to help you appreciate the fact that you have a second chance at life. You, however, may only be thinking about that sweet lady who used to be in the hospital bed next to you, with whom you had many long, comforting conversations about her kids, grandkids, cute dog, and all the things you both wanted to do when you were 'free' from illness. You are still alive and she is not. You are grateful for your life, but you're equally if not more upset that somebody else had to die.

You may even begin to believe that the wrong person died, and that it should have been you instead. This could also lead to you, either deliberately or subconsciously, punishing yourself. You might do this by not allowing yourself to have fun or laugh because you feel like you don't deserve it any more than the person who passed away.

No matter what you're feeling: You're not ungrateful, you're not overreacting. You're grieving in a way that not many people understand.

Like other types of grief, survivor's guilt may also cause you physical symptoms on top of the mental and emotional ones you may be going through. Nightmares, vivid flashbacks, difficulty sleeping or staying asleep, and waking up in a cold sweat are quite common among sufferers. You may also experience mood swings, irritability, and sudden bursts of anger. If you've ever heard about the effects of PTSD, you may recognize that these are all overlapping symptoms. There's a very fine, blurry line between PTSD and survivor's guilt, so I would highly recommend getting professionally diagnosed before making the final decision on what type of treatment you'll undergo.

Survivor's guilt (and the feeling that you shouldn't be alive) can very often lead to depression and suicidal thoughts. Please, if you're feeling like this, contact someone immediately, there are many helplines you can call and even some that you can simply text if you don't want to verbally speak to anyone.

If you feel ok enough to try out some self-help solutions, here are some for you to go through.

Allow Yourself to Grieve, Even When You Think It Isn't Justified

What does that mean? Why wouldn't you feel that your grief is justified? If you've become acquainted with someone and you lose them, you are going to feel grief over the lost part in your life. But what about someone you didn't know at all? Are you *allowed* to feel guilt? If you were witness to a mass shooting that resulted in many people losing their lives, you probably didn't know all or at least some of the victims at all. Yet, you still grieve for them. It may seem strange from the outside looking in, but to you, that could have easily been you. So allow yourself to grieve for the people who have passed. All grief is justified.

Try to Talk About or Write Down Exactly What Happened

To say this is going to be tough is a huge understatement: Revisiting your traumatic experience is the last thing you want to do, but it will be helpful for creating a little bit of distance between you and what happened. It can allow you to see more clearly that you being alive isn't going to change the past. If you had been dead, you just don't know what could have happened to the other person, they may have passed anyway. Having a good support system is crucial to getting through survivor's guilt. If you don't have friends and family that you can rely on, support groups are easily available. It may help even more to converse with people who have been through their own survivor's guilt.

Forgive Yourself

I mentioned something similar in the previous section. Forgiving ourselves is hard, but it is crucial. Unlike most other types of guilt while grieving, survivor's guilt makes you feel guilty simply for living. In order to get past it, you have to embrace the fact that you did survive and that you have a second chance at life.

Do Something Positive

Initially, this might be difficult. You're so overwhelmed by the thought of going out into the world and talking to strangers, feeling like you have to pretend to be ok so as to not make others uncomfortable. When you feel like you're ready, do some good out in the world. Donate to a charity, volunteer at a homeless shelter, an old age facility or a dog shelter. Recognize how you having lived through that experience led to those frail, abandoned, or less fortunate having just one week, day, or even hour being happy because of you. Doing this will help you become aware of the impact you as a singular person can have on others.

Guilty About Feeling Relieved

When you lose someone who's been ill for a long time, say with something like cancer or AIDS, you feel crushed. You feel heartbroken, or devastated. Or at least, you're *supposed* to, right? You're supposed to be going through the initial phases of grief; shock and anger, you're not supposed to be breathing a little easier or sleeping a little better at night.

Right?

Relief is the feeling of a burden being lifted from your life. Now, that's not to say your loved one was a burden, but their illness and the pain that it put them— and by extension, you—through was. Your loved one is no longer in pain and, whether you believe in an afterlife or not, it's normal to feel relieved about that. Although it is most common among those who have a loved one suffering with a terminal illness, it can also apply to those who have a loved one who is struggling with addiction, severe mental health problems, or even disabilities. If your loved one is in pain for a prolonged amount of time, the chances of you feeling a bit of relief when they're out of that pain is high.

On that note, however, it's super important to notice that feeling relieved doesn't, by any means, mean you wanted them to die. On the contrary, you wanted them to get better and be perfectly fine, if you could have your way. But you are still relieved that they don't have to go through excruciating torture, whether physical, mental, or emotional, every day.

If you were the person's caregiver up until their death, you might also feel relief from all the stress you went through. It does not make you a selfish person to feel relief that you don't have to wake up every morning wondering if this is going to be the last day you have with your loved one, or if they even made it through the night. It doesn't make you a selfish person to be relieved that you have some time to breathe and look after yourself, something you likely haven't been doing for a long time. It's not selfish. I say again, you're not relieved because the person is dead, you're relieved because both them and you finally have peace.

Keep in mind that humans are very complicated creatures. We don't feel things in absolute terms, for the most part. You don't have to *only* feel sadness and you don't have to *only* feel relief, you most likely will feel those things, along with a whole plethora of other emotions at the same time.

Unfortunately, feeling relief after a death is not very widely understood until you go though it yourself. A person who hasn't experienced it may not be able to comprehend how someone could feel *happy* after losing a loved one and may even judge them as being heartless or other harsh terms. That's why, for this type of guilt, it is recommended to begin your healing process on your own instead of talking to someone else. Unless, of course, you're sure that person understands you and will not cast any judgment. At least until you can put everything into words and adequately explain *why* you're feeling the way you are, instead of just feeling that way.

This again goes back to journaling. Using the usual techniques of writing stuff down in order to see them from a different perspective is great, although it may be a little harder to be completely honest. Often, this feeling of relief makes us feel ashamed, especially in the early stages, and sometimes that shame carries over to the point where you have a hard time even admitting it to yourself. It's the feeling that we're most likely to shove down and never talk about because we don't want anyone—including ourselves—to believe that we're some sort of emotionless monster. I don't mean to sound cliché, but there is a lot of truth to the statement that admittance is the first step to recovery.

Once you've managed to be completely honest with yourself and written everything down, go back and look at what you wrote. Objectively, are you justified in your relief? Remember what caused your loved one's death in the first place and how the past few months or years have been for both you and them. Your loved one may have been sick almost every single day, not only from the hell that is cancer, but the chemotherapy as well. You heard them moan in pain whenever they moved a certain way, saw the emotional pain they were going through from being in such a helpless situation. You felt panic well up inside you every time your phone rang because you were sure that would be the hospital telling you that they didn't make it. Now they don't have to feel any of that pain and you don't have to feel any of that stress. You're devastated, yes, but are you justified for feeling relief? You are.

There's also another type of relief you can feel when someone dies. Particularly when that person was abusive towards you or made your life terrible in some way. I mentioned previously about how cutting someone out of your life might make you feel grief, even though you know they weren't good for you, but what happens if that person dies? Along with any grief you may feel, you're also highly likely to feel a huge sense of relief. Again, feeling relief—even in this case—doesn't make you a bad person. Although in some more severe cases, it can be different, we usually don't wish death on anyone, even our abusers. It's part of being human. For the majority of us, we just want everyone to be better or we want them out of our lives, we don't want them to die.

Figuring out all our mixed, overlapping feelings can take time, so we need to be extra patient with ourselves. It can be confusing, but it's a normal part of the grieving process for a lot of people; don't ever feel like you're the only one who feels the way you do.

Worksheet #4

Difficult Questions

Fill in the following prompts:

The last time I saw my loved one was

_____.

How did I lose my loved one?

_____
_____.

The most difficult memory I have of them is

_____
_____
_____
_____.

The thing I miss the most about them is

_____
_____
_____.

I feel the saddest when

_____

_____.

After answering the above questions, rate the way you feel right now:

I feel:

- Sad
- Ok
- Scared

- Angry
- Happy
- Numb

- Guilty
- Tired

Other:

_____

_____.

Chapter 5:

365 Days of Self Care

Physical Self Care

Self care is a super important part of the healing and grieving process. When you're grieving (or in any other kind of troubled mindset) it can be quite tempting to stay in bed all day, because you can't imagine doing anything. Spending a day in bed every now and then is perfectly fine, it's relaxing, it helps you recharge so that you can tackle life again the next day. But doing it too often is detrimental not only to your physical health, but your mental and emotional health too.

It's important to practice some form of self care while you're grieving, otherwise you run the risk of making things worse for yourself in the long run. This could be in the form of poor health due to inactivity and bad food choices, and if you shut yourself in all day, every day, you're more likely to suffer from depression.

So what can you do to avoid that and heal in a healthy, positive way?

We're going to discuss ideas for four different types of self-care in this chapter: physical, mental, spiritual, and emotional. Each of these are equally important, but more than anything, they're also deeply personal. So see what suits you, tweak it to your preference, give it a try and see how you feel afterwards.

Let's start with the physical aspect.

Physical self care is probably the thing most people think of when they hear the words self care. People think of taking long, hot, bubble baths and sipping on a glass of wine while you have cucumbers over your eyes and opera plays on a nearby radio. It entails so much more than that, however. Physical self care is making sure you keep your body healthy, because you need it to work well to heal in other ways.

Here are some ideas for physical self-care:

Take a Long, Hot, Bubble Bath

Yes, I know. I used this as an example of a cliché, but there's a reason it's so popular. Even if you're not usually one to take baths, give it a try every now and then. Sitting in warm water for a few minutes can be both therapeutic and it can relax sore muscles and help soothe tension. Add some calming atmospheric elements like scented candles or a bluetooth speaker; drop in some bath salts, bubbles, or a bath bomb, and take a few moments to just be by yourself. If you want to go the extra mile, book yourself a spa day, do your own spa day at home by yourself, or call a friend or family member over to pamper yourselves together.

Maintain Basic Hygiene

It's so common for people to neglect the most basic of things when their world has been turned completely upside down. Try and put extra effort into maintaining your basic hygiene, even on the days that you can barely get out of bed. Brush your teeth, take a shower, brush your hair. That's it. Once you've done that, you can go straight back to bed if you so wish, but you'll likely not want to after getting ready for the day.

Make Sure to Eat Well

People respond to grief and stress differently when it comes to food. Some eat very unhealthy comfort foods all day because it makes them feel better, while others barely eat anything, if at all. Now, more than ever, it's important to maintain balance in your diet. Food is fuel, and if you give yourself too much or too little, it can have an effect on everything else in your life. Eating too much unhealthy foods can lead to high blood pressure and type two diabetes which, aside from being potentially life threatening in the future, can cause you a lot of unnecessary stress now—which is the last thing you need. The same goes for eating too little. Not eating enough food can cause your vital organs to weaken and slow down, which can also be life threatening. So, while it's perfectly fine to eat your favorite comfort food while you're grieving, just make sure that you're enjoying it in moderation.

Limit Caffeine and Alcohol

Both of these things are stressors, so while I'm not trying to force you off starting your day with a cup of coffee (I wouldn't be able to give up coffee entirely either), you should be mindful of how much you're drinking throughout the day. Consider making a note of how you feel after you drink it, both mentally and physically. The same goes for alcohol, although that's a bit more of a slippery slope when grieving than coffee is. Some people, who barely drank before, turn to alcohol every day during the grieving process because of the dulling sensation. This is dangerous, so try and catch it before it gets out of hand, or make sure that you have someone who cares about you and will call you out on it. On the other hand, it's important to drink a lot of water at any time, but especially while you're grieving.

Exercise

I know, when you're stressed out and feeling absolutely terrible, the last thing you want to do is drive to the gym and run a mile on the treadmill. When we don't feel like doing anything, often the first thing that we put off is exercise because it requires hard work on our part, plus it can be extremely tedious. There are many ways to get around these excuses though. Even just a small amount of exercise when you really don't want to get out of bed can have a major effect on you. Not to mention that there are so many ways of working out—a good number of which don't even feel like you're exercising—and it's easier than ever to find something you love and get moving. Here are some ideas for exercise:

- Go to the gym (or use whatever gym equipment you have at home)

- Go for a walk outside

- Ride a bike

- Go to a trampoline park

- Dance

- Follow a workout video (there are plenty online for free)

- Play a sport

- Go swimming

- If you're not feeling up for doing cardio on some days, try things like pilates and yoga

These are just a few suggestions, it's ultimately up to your preferences when it comes to getting yourself moving. If you find yourself more motivated with a partner, then ask a friend to join you. If you get too distracted by everything outside of the walls of your house, then stay home and try one of the many other ways to stay active.

Take a nap

Sometimes, everything can feel overwhelming and you can't even think about doing something productive without your body physically recoiling in disdain. Taking a power nap can help you reset and get back on track.

Know Your Limits

Or, more specifically, your new limits. Before your loss, you might have been the most productive person on the planet: Working eight hour shifts and still coming home, cleaning the house, and cooking elaborate meals for your family, all before heading off to the gym. While you're grieving, you may feel drained and tired after being awake for only a few hours. You need to understand that those are your limits "for the time being" and that you unfortunately can't do anything about it other than just respecting it and planning your life around it.

Keep a Schedule

Having a daily schedule for the basic things in your life (like showering and taking a nap) can give you a sense of structure in what's probably a really confusing and disorganized time. A schedule can be either time based or task based. Time based is where you say that at eight a.m., you're going to have breakfast, then at nine a.m.

you'll go for a walk. Whereas task based focuses more on just making sure that tasks get done throughout the day, no matter what in what order and at what time they happen. Try to keep a schedule for a while until it becomes ingrained in you.

Mental Self Care

What is mental self care?

Physical self care is mostly self explanatory, it's about taking care of your body, but what about mental self care? In essence, it's about making your mind healthy. This could mean equalizing anxiety, depression, and other stressors; or simply clearing your mind of all the mental clutter that is likely stocked up in there.

Mental self care is just as important to the grieving process as physical self care, if not more. You live and move based on what your head is telling you, so making sure that you're as mentally healthy as possible can help make the grieving process a little easier. This is not to say that if you practise good mental self care, you won't have any negative, unsettling, guilty, or intrusive thoughts at all. It's just to set you up to be more prepared to handle the self-defeating thoughts as they come your way.

Here are some ideas for mental self care:

Get Some Fresh Air and Sunlight

It's a widely known fact that something as simple as standing in a ray of sun and breathing in the fresh outdoor air can have a massive impact on your mental health. People who are cooped up in a dark room day in and day out experience more mental fog than if they were to simply open their curtains and windows. So, going outside to do some sort of activity is preferred, but just letting natural light in can also have a positive effect on your mentality.

Do Something That Requires Focus

Solve a rubix cube, a sudoku puzzle, or a jigsaw puzzle, something that will force you to concentrate on it for a certain period of time. If you like playing video games, play something that requires you to be skilled at it (especially if you're good at said game, the added rush of doing something well will boost your mood too).

Limit Your Social Media and News Intake

Social media can be fun, but it also often causes us stress for one reason or the other. Whether you happen to come across a thread of two people arguing that still ruins your day, despite the fact that you have nothing to do with it, or if you see someone directly saying bad things about your loved one—stressors can come in all forms and intensities on the internet. That's not to say you should become a digital hermit and not pay social media any attention at all, but rather limit the amount of time you spend online or select which sites and apps cause you the most stress and try not to open those as much as possible. The same goes for the news. Knowing what's going on around you is definitely important, but surrounding yourself with all the negativity that goes on in the world is not the best thing for your mental health. Keep up to date, but know when you've consumed enough.

Join a Support Group

Support groups are usually small groups of people who are going through similar experiences as you. At first, you might wonder why it's beneficial at all to get a bunch of grieving people together when you're all lost and probably can't offer each other good advice. But for many, grief makes you feel alone and isolated, so the thought of having others who—even though they may not know how to make you feel better—understand what you're going through. It's a huge source of comfort. Many of these groups also have counselors or people who have come through on the other side of grief, who can offer you some advice and insight, so try to find one in your area and consider going. Chapter seven of this book delves into support groups much deeper, so take a look at that and decide if you think it will be a good fit for you.

Take Note of the Voice Inside Your Head

This is the voice that tells you never to give up and to just push forward a little more, or it could be the voice that tells you to give up completely and that things are never going to get better. When we're grieving, our inner voice can turn negative, no matter how much of an optimist we are at heart. The first step to healing our shaken minds is to notice what it's saying to us. Is your thought process generally positive or negative? Are you subconsciously setting yourself up for a tough few months because your mind isn't being nice to you? Or maybe you're just living one day to the next, almost apathetic about the grieving process. Whatever is going on inside your mind, you need to know that it's there before you can address it in any way.

A simple way to do this is through meditation. We will discuss meditation more in depth in the next part, but one simple type of meditation is to sit in a silent room and close your eyes, allowing your mind to run free. Whatever pops into your head: Notice it, try to put it into words, and then let it go. By doing this, you'll begin to notice your thoughts and give them actual coherency. This way you can get a good idea of what the voice inside your head's general tone is.

Tell People How You Feel

This isn't just about telling them your inner thoughts and emotions, but also establishing boundaries. One of the hardest things to do as humans is to tell someone 'no'. We could be exhausted, both mentally and physically, but we'll still take on a task because someone asked us to, and we tell ourselves we *should* be able to do at least that. We don't want to disappoint people, especially those closest to us, but sometimes it's necessary. Believe it or not, the people that we're saying 'no' to are human too. So if we explain the way we feel and why, instead of just doing everything willingly at the moment, there's a high chance they'll understand.

Schedule Your Grief

I mentioned this technique earlier, but I feel like it's important to note here as well. Scheduling your grief means taking a few minutes out of your day to do nothing but worry and feel terrible. Throughout the day, if something pops up inside your head that bothers you, make a mental or physical note of it and tell yourself that you'll address it later. When later comes, give yourself a specific time frame to just let all the thoughts and feelings consume you. Don't concern yourself with trying to rationalize any of the thoughts during this time, just let them come and allow yourself to feel their full weight. Once your time is over, if you notice some thoughts that you can fix or rationalize, then make a plan on how to do that. If you can't fix the thoughts, then let them go; tell yourself you'll worry about them during tomorrow's grief schedule.

Take a Day off from Everything

We all need a day off every now and then to keep us sane. So every now and then, take a day off; not just from work, but from everything. Order takeout that day so you don't have to worry about dinner, allow your laundry basket to get just a little over full, don't bother to do your hair, just let go for a day. You can get back to life tomorrow, but for one day, just do nothing. It's like a spring clean for your mind.

Emotional Self Care

What is emotional self care?

Your feelings and emotions can dictate your everyday life just as much as your mental health can. Emotional self care is about connecting with your emotions and preventing the bad ones from getting out of hand on a regular basis.

When you grieve, your emotions can jump around minute by minute. You could feel fine and content one moment and be bawling your eyes out the next. Practicing emotional self care can help that switch to not be so harsh and intense and also give you that mood boost when you really need it.

Here are some ideas for emotional self care:

Feel Your Emotions

It's in our nature to try to push down and ignore any feelings that make us uncomfortable, but it's important to feel them, no matter how difficult that may be. Just like listening to your inner voice, the only way to understand your emotions is to feel them fully and unfiltered. It may also be useful to put your emotions in words. Just accept the way you feel at any given time. That's easier said than done, but every time you experience an unpleasant emotion, say to yourself, either internally or out loud, "Oh, I'm feeling *x emotion* right now," and stop there. Don't judge it, don't say you wish you weren't feeling like that, just feel it.

Smile and Laugh

Tricking ourselves into feeling a little better is very possible. Remember laughing yoga from chapter two? Well, something similar happens when we smile. Because we associate smiling with being happy, we can trick ourselves into feeling happier, even if it's just a little. If you need a little help with this, try watching a sitcom, or a funny movie, or a cat video on the internet. As long as it makes you smile, go for it.

Go on a Trip

Getting away from the same surroundings you see every day can make a big difference in your happiness levels. Plan a vacation with your family for a week at the sea, or spend a night by yourself in a nearby hotel. Just getting away will take you out of whatever rut you feel like you've been stuck in at home while you're grieving. Even if you don't spend an entire night away from home, simply going on a drive to clear your head and take in nature or the city streets is a literal and figurative breath of fresh air.

Immerse Yourself in Entertainment

If you're a bookworm, read a book. If you're a movie buff, watch a movie. If you have a musical soul, listen to music. Whatever form of entertainment most speaks to you. You may have to be extra careful about the type of movies you watch, books you read, and music you listen to as many things may trigger your grief without you even realizing they would. That isn't inherently a bad thing; sometimes it's easier to work through difficult feelings while doing something you enjoy, so don't shy away from the tougher subjects if you feel like you're ready. Above all, be kind to yourself and don't put yourself through unnecessary pain.

Listening to music, in particular, can be healing. Listening to songs that suit your mood can help you feel less alone. It might seem weird to feel connected to a song or to the writer of that song, but trust me, it isn't. When you grieve, you're looking for someone to understand you, and if those song lyrics seem to match you perfectly, then it only makes sense that you feel connected to it. After all, someone out there wrote those lyrics, so someone out there must have felt very similar to how you do right now. So sing along and allow yourself to feel connected to the song.

Care for Something

If you have a pet, show it extra love and care—and be sure to cuddle with it if you can. If you don't have a pet, get a small plant. Whatever you have, nurture it and care for it. When we raise something other than ourselves, we feel a sense of being needed, along with love for our dependents. Yes, you can get as attached to a plant as you can to an animal. Watching something grow and evolve is also massively satisfying and gives us a boost of pride.

Even if you don't have the time or patience to raise something yourself, for some animal lovers simply spending time with a cute, fluffy creature can boost your mood. So go to your friend's house just to play with their dogs, or go to a petting zoo, or, if you're lucky enough to live in an area with a cat cafe, go spend a few hours eating dessert and petting kitties. Animals have an effect on many of us that we just can't deny.

Talk to Someone

I know, I sound like a broken record at this point—but having good, supportive people around you while you're healing is so important. Did you know that just chatting with someone counts as self care? That's one more reason to pick up the phone and call your friends and family. If you have the chance to meet up, don't underestimate the power of human contact. A three second hug can make you feel comforted and cozy for hours afterwards, so hug people.

Quickly, while I'm on the subject of things I've spoken about a hundred times already, journaling is also a form of emotional self care.

Revamp Yourself and Your Space

That could mean spring cleaning your house, rearranging the things on your desk, or cutting your hair. A change is necessary from time to time and, if you can't get out of the house, then make the house work for you by changing or upgrading the aesthetics. The way our surroundings look can influence how free or stuffy we feel, so take a look around you and see if maybe something is suffocating you without you even noticing.

Do Something Creative

If you like to paint, then get out the paint and the canvas and have at it. You don't have to paint something that pertains to your grief or your feelings (feel free to, if you want); just doing something that you're good at and that you enjoy can boost you up.

Obviously, it doesn't have to be painting. Writing, drawing, dancing, singing, playing an instrument—as long as you're enjoying yourself and being creatively stimulated by it, go for it.

Do Something Good for Others

We've all heard the saying 'there is more happiness in giving than in receiving', and that is definitely true for a lot of us. Volunteering or donating to a good cause is one of the biggest mood boosting things you can do. Especially if you can see the impact your generosity is having on other people. You don't even have to physically *give* anything. Just a word or two can make someone's day and make the world feel like a better place for those few moments. So whether it's walking an old lady across the street or complimenting your coworker on how her hair looks today, putting a smile on someone's face is sure to put one on yours too.

Meditate

There are many different ways to meditate, I briefly touched on one in the previous section. Mindfulness meditation is one of the most popular self care meditations these days. I'm not going to go too in depth here, but here's a basic overview of how to do one such meditation:

1. Sit or lie down comfortably and close your eyes.

2. Breathe in for six counts, hold for four, and then exhale through your mouth for eight counts.

3. Repeat that three times.

4. Let your breathing go back to normal.

5. Focus only on your breaths. Tune out the world around you as best you can and focus inwards. You can mentally count your breaths if it makes it easier to focus (count one when you breathe in, then two when you breathe out, then repeat).

6. Your mind will begin to wander, when this happens, notice it, don't judge yourself for it, and then simply bring your attention back to your breaths.

7. Do this for as long as you wish.

8. When you're done, simply open your eyes and go on with your day.

The point of mindfulness meditation is to bring you back to the present moment. We spend so much time worrying about the future or ruminating on the past. These meditations start out as a way to give you some peace for the few minutes that you do it, but over time you may be able to ground yourself in the present at random times throughout the day without needing to do the entire meditation. It's also common to start out only being able to do anywhere from one to five minutes before getting antsy. This is completely normal and you'll be able to meditate for longer once you've done it more times. Try it out.

Spiritual Self Care

What is spiritual self care?

In essence, it's about fulfilling your soul and cleansing your spirit. It's also about connecting with something bigger than yourself, be that God, the universe, or even nature. Spiritual self care can be religious, but it also doesn't have to be. Since religions differ in practices, each faith has its own ways of healing and self care, so do whatever feels right for you.

Here are some ideas for spiritual self care:

Yoga

Yes, on its base level, yoga is strength training mixed with flexibility and stretching, but it's also deeply rooted in spirituality. The majority of yoga poses are meant to connect your body and soul with the earth, nature or another form of spiritual being. Yoga is a deep, vast practice that many swear by both for physical and spiritual benefits.

Meditation and Prayer

I know I spoke about meditation in emotional self care, but mindfulness meditation is not based on any spiritual practices, rather it's about grounding yourself in the moment. Meditation in the spiritual sense involves connecting with a higher power and obtaining a deeper meaning about life, the universe, or simply yourself. Spiritual meditation and prayer can be very similar in the sense that you're connecting with something bigger than the things you can physically see and touch. Many people find peace by doing this, and often feel like the higher power is taking some of the burden off of them.

Read a Spiritual Passage

This could be a scripture from the Bible, a passage from the Qur'an, or anything that has meaning to you or is comforting to you in the moment; anything that helps you move forward in your daily life, be that feeling like a higher power is watching over you. For the non-religious out there, reading experiences about how people connected with the universe may give you similar feelings of being watched over and nurtured by mother nature and the Earth.

Practice Gratitude

Practicing gratitude isn't inherently spiritual, but thanking the universe, God, or other deities for the little things in your life can help you feel more connected with the higher power. Thanking them for what you have can also help you notice and count your blessings, making you a more grateful and content person.

Speak with a Spiritual Advisor

A spiritual advisor is usually someone who shares your beliefs and can guide you to a stronger spirituality. This can be a pastor, a priest, an imam, or even someone non-religious who simply has a strong tie to spirituality like a psychic or a tarot card reader. Conversing with these people can help you figure out what steps to take to gain a deeper spirituality in yourself.

Attend a Religious Event

Most religions have weekly gatherings where followers worship freely in their venue. These can definitely be a huge source of spirituality for those who attend. Even if you're not religious, attending one of these events may give you a deeper idea as to how others perceive spirituality and it may even help you to shape your own personal version of what it means to you. So don't be afraid to attend a religious gathering, even if you don't have any intention of joining them, the experience alone could help you get closer to the higher power that you personally believe in.

Look to the Stars

This one isn't for everybody: Studying practices like astrology, horoscopes, magic, tarot, or other 'occult' practices can be equally as enriching. These are tools you can use (believe them factual or not) to understand how you, as an individual, process trauma.

Think of them like a reflective wall to bounce your thoughts off of—a house of mirrors, the deeper you tread. Astrology, for example, breaks down different aspects of a person's life in a multitude of ways: career, love, family, struggles, attitude, driving force—all the way down to personality traits. Obviously not everyone believes that distant constellations have anything to do with their lives, but even if you recoil at what's suggested about you from 'readings', it could be helpful to consider *why* that is. Sometimes our knee-jerk reaction tells us more than we think. It could also help you feel more connected to others and the universe. Reflecting on themes or ideas brought up in daily card draws can help you articulate your feelings, your habits, or patterns of thought—be they healthy or unhealthy.

Worksheet #5

Self Care

Try out at least one of the self care tips of each category (physical, mental, emotional, spiritual) and fill out the following:

What physical self care technique have you tried?

_____
_____.

How did you feel afterwards?

_____
_____.

What mental self care technique have you tried?

_____
_____.

How did you feel afterwards?

_____
_____.

What emotional self care technique have you tried?

_____
_____.

How did you feel afterwards?

_____
_____.

What spiritual self care technique have you tried?

_____
_____.

How did you feel afterwards?

_____
_____.

Chapter 6:

Preserving Memories

Remembering Them Fondly

When you lose someone close to you, you may, from time to time, feel so overwhelmed with loss and sadness that you think it'd be best if you somehow just managed to forget them altogether. Trust me, I can understand this sentiment. You want peace from all of your negative thoughts and feelings. If you just forgot about them, then you wouldn't have to deal with those feelings, right? I've been there. I even started wondering if there was a type of hypnosis I could have done to rewire my brain without having to do all the gritty, unpleasant work.

Or maybe you're not quite at that level. Maybe you've found yourself flip-flopping on a near daily basis between wanting to keep the person's memory alive inside you and wanting to erase them just temporarily so that you can get some relief from your grief. Whatever the circumstances are, it can be difficult to know how to keep someone's memory alive while still healing from your loss, and not letting it turn into an obsession.

It's important to note that the goal of the grieving process is not to forget the person, or completely detach yourself from them,]. That is an unreasonable demand to have. No matter who the person was, you had enough of a connection to them to grieve over losing them, so you're not going to be able to erase them from your life. The real goal of the grieving process is to come to terms with the new, long distance relationship you're now forced to have with them. Yes, when a person passes away, your relationship with them changes, it doesn't go away. It's a very common occurrence for people to talk about their deceased loved ones as if they're just on an extended trip somewhere far away. If you believe in an afterlife of some sort, many people spend time every now and then talking to their loved one, and even if you don't believe in it, you still maintain a relationship with that person after they're gone.

You may have seen people move on from a loved ones death very quickly and wonder why you can't do that. Or you may have even seen a family member move on from the same loss that has you stuck in a loop and you feel like you're the only one who still cares about the person. Keep in mind that, just like how everyone grieves differently, everyone memorializes a person differently too. Often, it's an automatic response that just happens over time and without much thought, but sometimes you do need a few ideas of how to do so.

So, what can you do to remember your loved one fondly?

Share Memories

Sharing memories about a person is the best way to keep them alive. Talk about the big things like how nervous they were on their wedding day, to the smallest things like that time the cat fell asleep on their face. The memories you have with this person are incredibly important. Trading stories with other people who knew them is another great way to remember them. Even though it's not your own personal memory of them, the fact that it's something that they did just adds one more memory to your memorialization bank.

You do have to be careful and show some discretion when sharing memories or just talking about the person in general, especially early on in the grieving process. This is because those wounds are still raw for you, and they may also still be raw for others. Make sure that it's an appropriate time to talk about that person and try and gauge the reaction of the person you're talking to. You wouldn't want to be forced to talk about something you're uncomfortable with, so try not to put others in those situations either. If you're met with outright hostility, just keep in mind that they're probably still in pain and give them their space. There's no timeline on when you have to talk about your memories of them.

Telling their stories to others is another great way of remembering them. Recount the stories they used to tell—that you've probably heard time and time again—

and pass those stories on by telling them to your kids, your friends, or anyone else that's close to you.

You could even share memories with someone who didn't know the person. Tell them about the little quirks they had, about what their favorite flower was, or how they were a great piano player, or had an eye for interior design. Tell them about things that you did with your loved one, or about the times you got into petty fights over food, or something like that. Just speaking about them is a form of memorialization.

Traditions

Likely, your loved one had their own rituals, traditions, and habits. This could be things like not eating meat on Fridays, or throwing a dinner party on the second Saturday of every month. By keeping these traditions alive, you keep a part of that person alive as well. You don't even have to do it exactly as they did, you could switch it up and tweak it to a point that suits you. For example, if your mother would spring clean on the first weekend of spring, you could insead choose to invite your siblings over every year on the first weekend of spring for lunch. Even though you're not doing the same thing that she was, you're still keeping the tradition of something happening on the first weekend of spring—and whether other people know it or not, you know where that tradition stems from, and that's all you need to remember.

Hobbies and Likes

Make your loved ones favorite food for dinner randomly one night. Watch their favorite movie during family movie night. If they liked to sew, try busting out a needle and thread, and try sewing a pocket onto something. If they enjoyed ice skating, grab a few friends and go to the ice rink this winter. If they were a fan of a certain singer or group, go to their concert next time they're in your town.

Engage in the things that your loved one liked doing. A lot of these things may not be appealing to you, but just the action of attempting something that was so dear to them is a way to remember them. You obviously don't have to force yourself to turn those things into your own hobbies and likes, but remembering them for those things can memorialize them rather effectively.

Give

Did your loved one have a specific charity that they gave to, whether it was an ongoing thing, or they were just moved one time to donate? Or did they have a cause that was close to their heart like protecting animals or taking care of the elderly? If they were a regular donator to a charity that was special to them, you can keep their memory alive by continuing to donate to that same charity or cause. If they weren't, you could donate to a charity of your choice in their name. Try to look for a reputable charity that deals with something that would have been dear to them.

If you would like a larger scale memorialization and want to give back to the community at the same time, you could start your own charity or grant in your loved ones name and use the money raised for a cause that you deem worthy.

Yearly Celebrations

Getting the family together on your loved ones birthday or the day they died is probably the most common way to remember them. You and your family and friends can decide on your own yearly memorial that works for everyone and that is dedicated to your loved one. Obviously, this doesn't mean that you *only* remember them on those specific days. Some people choose to set a place at the dinner table for their loved one every night and, in some cultures (if you drink alcohol) it's customary to pour a glass and leave it on the table for the deceased. Small gestures like that can also be a form of memorialization.

In my opinion, the worst thing we can do for someone who has passed away is to reduce them to just their death. They lived a life before that and focusing on that instead of how it ended is not only healing for us, but it's a much better way to remember them and keep them alive inside ourselves.

Ultimately, the best form of memorialization is to simply remember them.

Mementos and Pictures, Should You Keep Them?

Deciding which of your loved ones possessions to keep is rather tricky and, like everything else in the grieving process, personal to everyone involved. While it's generally not practical to keep every single thing that your loved one owned, there are some things that you can choose to keep as mementos.

So what kind of things can you keep?

The answer to that is: anything. Or more specifically, anything that has sentimental value of some sort. My grandmother used to have about 20 plastic butterflies decorating her bedroom wall and, before she passed away in the early 2000s, she made sure to designate each and every one of them to specific grandchildren. To this day, I still have the butterflies that were left to me in my own room. If you were to buy a whole pack of these in a store today, they'd probably be cheaper than a cup of coffee, but what gives them value is the sentiment. Those ones in the store might be butterflies, but they're not *my grandmother's* butterflies.

My point is that everyone has different things that they consider to be valuable, either to them or their loved one, so it's up to each person to decide what to keep and what not to.

Some of the most common mementoes that people keep are:

- Clothes (only certain items of clothing that have meaning to you)

- Homeware items like dishes, cutlery, tablecloths, certain appliances, etc.

- Jewelry

- Antiques and things that have been passed down within the family

- Trinkets that remind you of them like ornaments or a specific cushion

Of course, there are many things that are unique to your situation and perhaps the best way to decide what to keep and what to either donate or throw out, is to do it while the whole family is present. Getting rid of things that belonged to your loved one can be extremely difficult at times because it feels final, like you're getting rid of a part of that person. In that case, consider donating as much of it as you can, so that, instead of feeling like you got rid of it, you can know that you gave it to a good cause, and that can do so much better than if it was in your storage closet, collecting dust.

What about photos?

Most likely, *keeping* photos of a deceased loved one around isn't the question, it's whether or not you should put them on display for you, your family, and any visitors to see.

This again comes down to what feels right for you and your family. Some people react differently to photos of their loved ones, so if you want to display photos, be sure that everyone in your household is comfortable with that. If they or you don't feel ready yet, then you can always store the photos away and give yourselves time to process everything, before maybe attempting it a second time. Of course, you don't have to display them at all, it's a personal choice.

Displaying photos doesn't mean that you're holding on to the past and not moving forward by longing for what used to be. People like to keep photos of their loved one for a multitude of reasons.

That person is still dear to you, so you want to give them the respect they deserve by keeping their photo up. Taking them down and *not* displaying them could make you feel like you're erasing them. Some people also keep photos of their parents and grandparents up so that their children can become familiar with them and not see them as strangers. Many cultures and religions display the deceased's photo to honor them and some even create small altars inside the house for them.

When is it not a good idea to display photos?

Photos can be a trigger, either for you, your family, or even friends and relatives. If you do want to ultimately display their photo, but it's too hard for you to look at the person at the moment, then wait until you're ready. There's no set time for when you have to put your photos out on display. If your house is the site of a lot of traffic in the form of friends and family coming to visit, then it may be a good idea not to display the photos right away, as it might be triggering for those who come to your house. That's not to say that you should let other people dictate what you do, but if you know that someone who is visiting was highly affected by the death, then it would be nice to preemptively remove any photos, just in case.

Ultimately, if you want to put up photos and you feel like the time is right and your household is ok with it, then by all means, put the photos up. It's up to you.

Giving Their Memories a Special Place

Why do people buy headstones for their loved ones?

It might seem like just a socially accepted thing that everyone does, but there's a reason for it: it's physical. Having a headstone or any other kind of physical memorial like that gives you a place that you can go to remember your loved one. Of course, remembering your loved one doesn't *require* you going to their grave, but people often visit the grave to talk to them

Grave markers are only one type of physical memorial though. There are many other things you can use to memorialize your loved one:

An Item of Theirs

In keeping with the previous part, you can keep an item of clothing or an ornament of theirs as a physical memorial. You could keep the item safe in a glass case or have it encased in something like perspex to keep it from wearing over the years. You could even create a small shrine inside your home, if you feel like that is something that you want to do.

Trees

A special tree can memorialize a person. You could choose to plant a tree in your yard or in a public place, or you could even sponsor the planting of trees in your loved ones name. It doesn't even have to be a huge tree, just planting something small like a vegetable plant in your backyard could be a memorial to them. Think of it as that plant being *their* plant. If your loved one was cremated, some people like to place the ashes in a biodegradable box, plant something, and plant the box with the tree. You can look at it as your loved one helping that tree to grow.

Crafts

If you have a special connection to certain items of clothing that your loved one wore but you have no intention of wearing it yourself, you can use those items of clothing to create something. It could be anything from a teddy bear to a cushion cover to a patch quilt. Think of it as a way of keeping your loved one's items in a way that will be more practical in your life. It doesn't even have to be something of theirs, you could make a collage of their photos or, if you're into pottery, create something in honor of them.

Tattoos

Tattoos are not for everyone, but if you want to do it, then having a memorial tattoo is a very personal, very beautiful way to memorialize somebody forever. Some people get the person's name tattooed, some get their portrait, some get their birth and death dates, and some get something that has significance to that person—like their favorite flower, or the quote they used to say all the time. If you're getting any tattoo, but especially if you're getting one as important as that, make sure you go to a reputable tattoo artist.

Jewelry

It's also possible to have ashes turned into beautiful jewelry. This is another great way of both memorializing your loved one and keeping them close to you at all times. The most common type of jewelry that people have made this way is pendants, but you can get other types like rings and earrings made too.

Online Memorial

We live in the age of technology, so creating an online space for family and friends to visit and comment could be a good idea; especially if you have family that live far away from either you or your loved one's final resting place. You do have to be careful about online memorials. Be sure to make it private and that everyone who joins has to be vetted by you or someone close to you first. Online memorials are great, but unfortunately the internet is filled with trolls, so you have to take those measures to prevent any harm from being done.

The type of memorial—or if you even have a physical memorial in the first place—is entirely up to you, and is also incredibly versatile. This list was just a few things that you could do, but everyone's circumstances and everyone's story is different, so do whatever feels right for you.

Worksheet #6

My Loved One

Write down your favorite memories, funniest memories, or any random facts about your loved one.

_____

_____

_____

_____

_____

_____

_____

_____

Part 3:

September - December

Chapter 7:

Sharing Without Shame

You Can Get Stuck While Grieving Alone

Feeling 'stuck' is something that some of us might experience a little further into the grieving process.

I want to give you an analogy: If you've ever tried to learn a language, you might start by reading some books, going to a website, or downloading an app. These textbook style learning devices give you a great basic knowledge of the language and you may get to a point, after a while, where you can read and write many useful sentences in that language. But then, you attempt to speak or listen in your target language and you realize that you're nowhere near fluent. That's because you haven't had conversations in that language yet, so you haven't gotten used to all the nuances, slang, and pronunciation. If you choose to keep studying by yourself, instead of talking to native speakers and immersing yourself in the language, you're going to get 'stuck' and not know how to move forward, no matter how much you want to do so.

Getting stuck in grief is obviously a lot more serious than not being able to speak a language fluently, but it's a similar principle: If you try to do it completely on your own, you're likely to get stuck.

What Does Getting Stuck in Grief Entail?

Of course, when you're grieving you're going to feel very intense and unpleasant emotions, especially at the beginning. Those feelings lighten over time, but you can get to a point where it feels as if you've been at the same spot in your grief for an extended period of time. Keep in mind that feeling 'stuck' and feeling like you're spiraling deeper into grief are two different things. If it feels like you're getting worse over time, you should…? That's right, consult a professional near you, as that could be an indication of depression.

Feeling stuck means that you're not quite at the point of acceptance with your life, but you've hit a wall and don't know how to get past it. It's also different from unresolved grief in the sense that unresolved grief comes from a conscious choice to push your feelings down and attempt to ignore them, while feeling stuck comes from having a desire to heal, but not knowing where to go from where you are.

I kind of touched on this in my analogy, but one of the easiest ways to get stuck in grief is by keeping everything inside and not talking to others about it. Isolating yourself both emotionally and physically can make you feel more and more stuck, and you may start to believe that you're never going to get past this hurdle—that you'll feel like this for the rest of your life.

Of course, everyone has their own reasons for not opening up and talking. You could be a shy person who doesn't open up often. You might not know what to say, have a fear of being judged, or just don't have the energy for people at the moment. You might also feel like what you're feeling isn't as intense, and therefore not as important, as someone else's grief. We've all heard how *x person* has it worse than us, and that can cause us to believe that our feelings and struggles are invalidated because our lives are not as bad as theirs.

As a little side note; never let anyone tell you that your grief 'isn't as bad' as someone else's. Everyone feels things differently and if you feel like you're struggling with grief while someone who was even closer to the deceased seems to be doing fine, that doesn't invalidate your feelings at all.

How Grieving with Others Helps You to Feel Unstuck

The hopeless feeling of being stuck in grief can be terrible and even frightening, but you don't have to go through it alone.

There are three main avenues that you can go down when looking for someone to share your grief with:

- Friends and family

- Counselors and therapists

- Support groups

Let's discuss each one of those avenues.

Friends and Family

This one is quite self-explanatory and it's been at the core of everything I've spoken about in this book so far: Having a trusted companion (or more than one) who you can pour all your feelings out to, and who will listen to you and give advice whenever you need—it's perhaps the most ideal support system that you can have. However, you face the possibility of putting too much pressure on one single person and they might not know what to say or how to help you. They may also begin to think that you only see them as a person that they can rant to instead of someone whose relationship is important to you, so you have to use your discretion and be mindful about your support system's feelings as well.

If you can find that perfect balance, then just talking with a friend or someone else close to you can help you get past the giant wall that you're currently stuck facing.

Counselors and Therapists

Firstly, what's the difference?

Those two terms are often used interchangeably, but there is a difference. Although, it could be different depending on where you are, in general, *'counseling'* is about helping you get your life back on track and deal with day to day life in a healthy way while you're grieving; while *'therapy'* is important when your grief becomes too intense to handle or you begin to develop additional issues such as anxiety and depression on top of your grief. However, as I said, some people use those two terms interchangeably, so make sure, if you choose to seek out professional help, that you know what kind of help they're offering.

One-on-one sessions, whether with a counselor or a therapist, is not a quick solution for your grief—as much as you might hope it would be. It's just there to help steer you in the right direction and give you a little push, especially if you're feeling stuck and unsure of what you can try to help you move forward. Counselors and therapists provide outside insight, and give you tools that you have to apply in your day to day life.

It may be in your best interest to seek out a therapist or counselor if you're having feelings of guilt and are too afraid or ashamed to talk to anyone else. These sessions are completely private and you can talk about anything to your therapist, so if you're struggling with guilt and need someone to talk to, maybe try contacting a reputable therapist near you.

Therapists could also assess you to make sure that you're not dealing with something else other than grief such as trauma, PTSD, or anxiety. If you just need someone to vent to in order to feel better, then contact a counselor.

Support Groups

Sometimes we don't have anyone to talk to, and feel like we are not being heard or understood. We struggle to talk to those closest to us and instead find it easier to open up to strangers. If this is the case with you, then support groups might be the thing to try. Support groups are about exchanging stories. The people in support groups are all in different phases of their grief recovery, so those who are further along can help those who are still struggling at the beginning by instilling a sense of hope that it will eventually get better, if only just a little.

Support groups are usually rather specific in the type of loss that they deal with. For example, you could have divorce support groups, illness support groups, as well as bereavement support groups. Within the bereavement umbrella, you also get different groups that cater to losing a loved one in specific ways. There could be a group specifically for those who have had a miscarriage, those who have lost a loved one to suicide, addiction, cancer—the list goes on. This is another thing that makes support groups work for some people, because who is going to understand you better than someone who is dealing with a very similar loss to you?

Certain support groups are led by qualified professionals, while others are led by people who have been through a similar situation and can relate to what you're going through. The groups with a professional at the head may focus more on activities and tools to help the group members move forward and deal with their grief, while those with one of your peers at the head may be more focused on community and a sense of understanding and togetherness.

One of the main draws of support groups is that they help you realize that you're not alone in the way that you're feeling, despite how much it may feel like the rest of the world is going on without any cares, while you're still grieving. You don't have to feel like you're boring the other people or that you're "being a downer". Nobody in a grief support group will judge you for grieving. Having that sense of camaraderie lets you get some of the burden that you're carrying off your shoulders.

If you feel like you want something more intensive, or that you would benefit from taking some time away from your current day to day life, there is also a type of support group that does that. These are called grief retreats, and many people swear by them.

Grief retreats are essentially resorts or pensions that are set up specifically for people who are grieving. They work on a set timetable, so they're not as flexible and easy to join when you need to as regular support groups. They take you away from your busy life for a while, usually to somewhere serene and beautiful, and allow you to focus on healing where you don't have any responsibilities. It's like a vacation but specifically catered to those who are dealing with loss.

Like support groups, there are grief retreats for different types of loss. These retreats also give you the chance to socialize and connect with others who are in a similar situation, but the majority of these retreats also include activities and workshops to help you connect with yourself and face your grief in a healthy way, even after you go home. They can be anywhere from one weekend to an entire two or three weeks, depending on the place you choose.

Ultimately, you getting 'unstuck' is entirely up to your actions and mindset, but being with other people—especially people who understand you—can definitely have a positive impact on you getting to that point.

How to Choose a Support Group for Your Grief

In the current day and age, the easiest and most efficient way to find a doctor, a dentist, or even a restaurant that serves a very specific cuisine, is by searching for it on the internet. It's no different for support groups. Sure, you can get referred to a support group by your doctor or by a good friend, but if you're looking for a group that deals with your specific type of loss without having to travel incredibly far every week, then checking online is the best way to go about doing that.

If you find a place that looks like it has everything you need, make sure of a few things first. Before you attend your first meeting:

Make Sure the Group is Reputable

Unfortunately, the biggest con for going online is that not everything can be taken at face value, so you have to make sure that the group is reputable and not just trying to scam you out of your money. Searching the group's name, looking at their website, and seeing what other people have to say about them—whether that's through reviews, or maybe you manage to find a story about someone's experience at the group on a forum or a blog—can let you know whether a place is really legit.

Make Sure the Location is Near You

You might find a really nice place far away and you could tell yourself that you don't mind driving there once a week, but you're going to have days where you don't want to do anything and you feel overwhelmed. If the place is close to you, you're much more likely to just go there instead of dreading a long drive. Of course, if you have the motivation to keep driving to a faraway group, that's great—but my recommendation is to go with something closer to where you live.

Make Sure Their Meeting Times Work for You

These support groups are supposed to help you heal, not add more stress to your life. So if you don't like going out after the sun goes down, then opt for a group that meets up in the morning or the afternoon. Of course, you may unfortunately not get the luxury of deciding what times you want to meet up if there's a lack of support groups in your area, but if you can, opt for what is the most comfortable to you. After all, you don't want to be stressed about having to wake up early if you're not a morning person, or stressing about how you're going to drive home in the dark if you have night blindness.

Make Sure You're Comfortable with the Group Size

Again, these groups are supposed to help you and be comfortable enough for you to let your guard down and open up. Some people like smaller groups where it feels like everyone has ample amount of time to talk about their loss, while others feel uncomfortable in small groups and prefer having more people around to avoid feeling singled out. Think deeply about what you would be ok with and what would bother you when it comes to the amount of people in a group, and make your decision from there.

Make Sure the Group is Run by a Qualified Therapist

As I said before: Not all groups are run by professionals. But if you're looking for one that's a bit more structured and focused on providing helpful ideas, then you might want to try looking for a group with a therapist at the head. Since this is still on the internet, it could add another layer of digging around to make sure that the person really is qualified—although most qualified therapists either display their qualification online and won't hesitate to prove it.

Make Sure the Group is/isn't Religious

Just like how you get groups for different types of grief, you also get groups that are based on specific religions. If you're not religious, then make sure the group you're looking at isn't religious either. You don't want to be put into a situation where you're the outsider. If you are religious, then do some digging to make sure that the group's core religious beliefs are in line with yours and that you'll feel comfortable there.

No matter how much research you do, however, you won't truly know if a group is right for you unless you attend one or two meetings. If you feel uncomfortable at any point, feel free to not go back to that group. Remember, this is for your own well-being. You're not obligated to do or say anything you don't want to, and if you feel like you're being put on the spot, bullied, heckled, or anything of the sort—walk out. You could also come across a situation where the group as a whole is really warm and comforting, but there's one person among them that just brings everybody down and makes you feel like you're wasting your time or that you're never going to move on from the grief that you're feeling. Again, think about yourself and walk out. That specific group isn't for you, and that's ok, you could try something else instead: A different group, one-on-one counseling, or even online group sessions.

Online Support Groups

Yes, support groups don't have to be face to face, in-person meetups. You can do just about anything online, and this is no exception. If none of the nearby in-person support groups worked for you, appealed to you, or if you're just more comfortable staying at home and connecting with people through the internet, then you should definitely give online support groups a try.

Since you can join online groups from wherever you live, even if it's overseas, you can choose to join the highest rated ones so that you know you'll have the best service available. It's also easier to find the specific topic of grief you're looking for if you're not restricted to a specific area, so that could be beneficial to you as well.

Another big selling point of online groups is that you're usually not required to turn your camera on at all, and this can be a very big plus point for people who find it hard to get themselves looking presentable on a daily basis, whether that's due to their grief or something else.

Of course, as with the face-to-face groups, you'll need to do some research on the online groups to make sure that they're legitimate and the right fit for you. If you do find something that works for you, then stick with it—whether it's in person or over the internet, grief support groups can help you immensely.

Worksheet #7

Putting Your Grief Into Words

Imagine that you have just joined a support group. Write down how you would introduce yourself, and tell a story about your loss.

_____

_____

_____

_____

_____

_____

_____

Chapter 8:

Learning to Escape, Defying Myths, and Getting Better

Grieving Myths to Avoid

Grieving is one of the most universally familiar among humans, so there's naturally going to be a lot of opinions about what is right and wrong; and with it, there's also bound to be many myths. These could be a product of what people have told you, what you've seen or read about, or just some misconceptions that you may have developed along the way due to things like your upbringing or your outlook on life. So, to try and tie things up in a nice little bow, let me tell you about some of the most common myths and what the truth actually is.

Myth: You Have to be Strong

You've probably been told to be 'strong' by somebody who really had the best of intentions, but what does 'being strong' actually mean? Adopting a "fake it until you make it" attitude can help with many things in your life (work, lifestyle, changing a habit or personality trait), but grieving is not one of those things. Being strong usually means that you're putting on an act—a strong front—and pushing down any 'weak' feelings that may arise. Doing this can lead to avoidance, which, as you know by now, is possibly the single worst thing you can do while grieving.

Myth: The End Goal of Grieving is to Feel Completely Back to Normal

Unfortunately, this is an unrealistic expectation, as much as you want it to be true. You've lost something incredibly important to you, so there's no way that things will ever be the same as they used to be. The goal of going through the grieving process is to learn how to effectively move forward with your life with the 'cards' that you've been dealt; as well as how to live with this new, different relationship that you now have with your loved one.

Myth: You Shouldn't Still be Grieving

Placing a time limit on grief, usually based on others' experiences, is a bad idea all around. I've said this many times throughout the book: Everyone grieves at their own pace, so some might feel better sooner than others. Yes, this book is called *365 Days of Grief Comfort*, but you'll notice that I mentioned right at the beginning of the book that it's not 365 days to recover. Instead, 365 days is generally enough time to begin putting all the grief techniques into practice and be on your way to moving forward with your life. Side note here: It's also important to remember that, even though people might seem like they're doing ok a week, a month, or a few months after a loss, that doesn't necessarily mean that they are ok. So the next time you ask yourself, "*x* moved on so quickly, why can't I?" Keep in mind that you don't know how they're really feeling on the inside.

Myth: Time Heals all Wounds

So, this one is partly true. You do in fact need a good amount of time to heal—I'm not disputing that at all—but what you do during that time can make all the difference. For example, if you choose to ignore your feelings and push them down every time they pop up, and you do this for years on end, you're not going to heal no matter how long you wait. Time will not heal you if you don't actively work on healing yourself as well.

Myth: Men Don't/Shouldn't Grieve

This is a weird one, but I have heard it before. There are a small group of people who seem to believe that men don't feel any emotional pain. I don't think I have to tell you how untrue that is. What's more common is the belief among men that they have to be strong for everybody around them. A lot of men are taught from a young age that they have to be tough, and that showing emotion makes them 'weak' or even 'girly'. It's unfortunate because men *do* feel grief—intense, debilitating grief in some cases—and should be encouraged to express it in a healthy way, just as women are.

Myth: I Shouldn't Talk About My Loss Because it Will Ruin the Mood

Talking to people is one of the best ways to deal with your grief, but you could definitely come across as a 'downer', especially if the atmosphere is generally happy. However, if you have a good support system around you—or even just a good friend—they'll be there for you no matter what. If the roles were reversed, you wouldn't see them as a burden, so try not to see yourself as a burden either.

Myth: Grieving and Mourning are the Same Thing

Grief refers to the feelings you have after experiencing a loss. It's entirely personal to you, and everybody feels it differently. Mourning is the *outward expression* of that grief.

Myth: I Shouldn't Talk About My Loss Because it Makes me Feel Terrible

Sometimes, especially when the wound is still raw, talking about it can be incredibly painful. You may actually feel better when you *don't* talk about it. Of course, this is a type of avoidance. As we know, the only way to really get through that pain and reach a point where talking about your loved one becomes less painful, is to go straight through it.

Myth: Talking About Your Loved One Years Later Shouldn't Upset You

If it's been years and speaking or hearing about your loved one still makes you emotional, you might think that means that you didn't grieve properly or that you've become stuck in your grief. Remember: The person is still dear to you, no matter how much time has passed, so you're going to miss them terribly sometimes—especially when talking or thinking about the times you spent together. You can still long to go back from time to time. That doesn't mean that you're stuck. It means you still care.

Myth: If You Don't Cry, it Means You Aren't Sad

You know those people who somehow *don't* scream on roller coasters? They're just not the screaming type; it doesn't come as a natural response to fear like it does for others. It's the same for crying: Some people just dont cry easily, or even at all, in some cases. Crying is a type of mourning—an outward expression of grief—so if you don't mourn by crying, that doesn't lessen the pain of grief that you feel. It's important to note that there's a difference between not crying and not *allowing* yourself to cry. Not allowing yourself to cry falls under the myth of having to be strong, as it's an avoidance behavior.

Myth: You Should Only Grieve Over the Death of a Loved One

You might have the misconception that unless you're grieving a loved one's death, you have no legitimate reason to grieve, and you're just being overdramatic. But you can grieve over anything that was important to you, whether that be a relationship, an inanimate object, or even just an idea. You grieve loss. Loss of a marriage, loss of a house, loss of dreams and ambitions. If something important is taken away from you, it will hurt you immensely.

Myth: Once You Start Feeling Better, it Will Only get Better from There

If the goal of the grieving process is to get to a point where not everything makes you feel utterly devastated. Then, once you start feeling better, that's mission accomplished, right? Well, no. Grief is a winding road, full of twists, turns, and alleys that pop up out of nowhere. Nothing is linear in grief. One day you might feel perfectly fine, ready to take on anything the world throws at you, and the next you feel like you're back to square one and everything hurts all over again. Overall, it will get easier, but there will be days that are harder than others.

Myth: If Your Loved One Passed at an Older Age/if You Knew in Advance, Your Grief Won't be That Bad

You might tell yourself or you might hear from other people that your loved one lived a full life and so you shouldn't be sad that they get to rest now. Similarly, you might lose someone due to an illness where you knew in advance that they wouldn't survive it, so you shouldn't feel bad when they're now at peace. You yourself might even believe those things, but you still find yourself grieving. This is normal. Removing someone who meant a lot to you from your life is bound to have an effect on you, whether they lived a full life, or you believe it was for the best or not. You have every right to feel sad.

Myth: If I Laugh or Start Having Fun Soon After Losing Someone, It Means I Didn't Really Love Them

As I said, you will have good and bad days during the grieving process. Sometimes those good days will come very soon after the loss, and the fact that you're not sad all the time might make you think that you didn't love the person enough. You think that you should feel grief at all times because they were so important to you and they're not here. Rest assured, you can love someone with all your heart and still smile and laugh as early as their funeral—I'll talk more about this in the next part.

Think about what your loved one would want for you, most likely they would want you to be happy.

Myth: If You're Religious and Feeling Grief, It Means You Don't Have Enough Faith in God

Many people believe that their deceased loved ones are in a better place and/or that it was God's plan for them to go when they did. However, those who believe this still feel pain from the loss and that's perfectly reasonable. Grief is a human emotion, no matter what we believe. The fact that we're experiencing such a huge change in our physical lives is what causes us to grieve.

Myth: Therapy is Definitely Going to Help You, and Quickly

Firstly, I have to stress this again, there is no "getting over it", it's only about getting more accustomed to your new way of life. Secondly, therapy can help, but it might not be for everybody. Some people just don't take well to therapy, while others don't need therapy at all and prefer to heal on their own with their own personal support system.

Myth: Keeping a Journal is Definitely Going to Help You

As much as I advocate for writing things down and journaling, and as much as it can help you to do so, journaling is not for everybody. Some people don't like writing, and even if you do, it can start to feel like a chore that ends up causing you more stress, which is counter intuitive to healing. If you don't like writing, you could actually keep a voice diary instead, or you could choose not to keep any kind of journal.

You Should Escape Sometimes

There's nothing wrong with escaping from your grief from time to time; in fact, it's encouraged to escape when things get too difficult. Even if you're grieving in a healthy way, grief can get overwhelming fast and you need to take a break from it every now and then. Now, you might be thinking, "Isn't that just avoiding the grief? Isn't that a bad thing?" and the answer is both yes and no. Yes, you're avoiding grief, but only for a short period of time, just enough for you to breathe and relax a little. It's not the same as deliberately not addressing your feelings at all. Just a few hours, or even a day or two, could provide the escape you need in order to recharge and get back to facing reality again. Even those who are not experiencing grief need an escape every once in a while, so how much more so would a grieving person?

So, What's an Escape?

An escape can be anything that appeals to you and takes your mind off everything going on in your life for a little while. The goal is to feel relaxed, calm, and in the moment.

You could mentally escape, physically escape, or both.

A mental escape is where you stay where you are, but escape from everything by focusing your mind on something that brings you joy for a few minutes or hours. Mental escapes can be done everyday, if necessary and are a great, easy way to destress.

Examples of a mental escape would be things like: getting engrossed in a movie or a series, playing video games, or reading a book. You could also do something creative like drawing, sculpting, panting, woodworking, or anything else that requires focus.

A physical escape is where you actually *escape* from your daily life and routine. This could be as simple as taking a day off from work and staying in your pajamas all day, to something as large as flying overseas for a nice island getaway. As long as it takes you away from the day to day stressors and gives you some relief from your grief for a little while, anything can be an escape.

Of course, you do get unhealthy escape practices, such as turning to drugs or alcohol. These things are particularly bad for you while you're grieving because you are more likely to develop a dependence on something while you're vulnerable. Get hooked on taking an hour out of your day instead to watch an episode or two of your favorite show, or get hooked on having to watch the sunset everyday, rather than something that's potentially destructive.

How Often Should You Escape?

As often as you need, is the simple answer. Everyone's different: Some people can take more of a beating from life and grief before they feel like they need a break, while others have a lower breaking point. If you feel overwhelmed by your grief, try escaping for a little while. If you continue to feel overwhelmed for an extended period of time, or you get worse, then seek out a professional. You may unknowingly be dealing with something other than grief, as well.

You could escape every day by doing some sort of mental escape for an hour or two, then maybe every weekend by going on a long drive and taking in the sights around you, or you could take a mini-vacation every month and go to a nice resort or hotel. Whatever you choose to do, as long as it works for you and you feel calm during—and hopefully after—then do whatever you need to.

Just be careful that your escapes don't turn into avoidance. It can be easy to want to escape whenever you feel any amount of grief, and I understand the desire to not go have to go through all the terrible thoughts and feelings that grief brings with it, but it's important to go through your grief head on and only escape after a specific period of time or when things become too much.

How to Laugh Through Your Grief

Laughing and grief are not generally two words that you think would go together, but it's actually to the contrary: They complement each other pretty well in a number of ways. The first is what many people call nervous laughter (or laughing in situations that seem inappropriate), and the second is using humor to get through something difficult. Let's take a look at both of these things.

Nervous Laughing

There are two types of people: Those who laugh in uncomfortable, terrible situations, and those who don't (and possibly also think that the former are crazy). You may have seen someone talk about how someone close to them has a life-threatening illness, or even that they passed away, all while keeping a smile on their face. Or they may even finish telling you about how scared they are about something serious and end their statement with a small laugh. 99% of the time, these people are not smiling or laughing because they're genuinely happy about the events or find it amusing. Instead, it's actually an automatic coping mechanism. You smile or laugh to try and make something seem not as bad, to 'soften' the blow. Although for many of us, we don't even think about it. It's just a subconscious way of disarming anyone you may be talking to or calming yourself down a little.

If you're not one of these people, you may actually think that they're being rude, disrespectful, or even heartless by laughing during something so terrible. But I urge you to understand that they don't mean any harm; it's often out of their control and is just an ingrained way that they deal with things that make them nervous, uncomfortable, sad, or even angry.

Deliberate Humor

Cracking jokes at a funeral seems like a super disrespectful thing to do, doesn't it? Well, it doesn't always have to be that way. Many people add little funny experiences in their eulogies, and in some cultures, it's customary to sing and dance joyfully at a funeral. Humor and laughing are some of the best ways to get through the worst of times. Of course, that's not to say that you should go up to a grieving widow and make some kind of off-color joke to her. Use your discretion when it comes to with whom you joke and the content of that joke.

Deliberate humor is different from nervous laughter, as nervous laughter isn't about humor at all. Nervous laughter is an automatic response to stress while deliberate humor is just that; deliberate. You may notice this in times of high stress and anxiety, for example, if you're stuck in an elevator with some incredibly claustrophobic people. You or those around you might make a joke to try and lighten the mood, especially if everyone else seems terrified.

Whether you're a nervous laughter or make a lot of jokes, the act of laughing can be very healing during the grief process. Remember laughing yoga? While laughing genuinely is better, even if you force yourself to laugh, it can send a signal to your brain to feel better and relieve stress. Apart from relieving stress, laughing can also elevate your mood, allow you to think clearer, put things into perspective (you'll see things for what they are instead of as a huge, imposing mountain), and it can even alleviate physical pain as well. Laughter could also be one of the healthiest forms of escapism, and it's something that you can do multiple times a day to help you feel better without it turning into avoidance.

But how do you genuinely laugh when you're in pain?

You have likely made hundreds if not thousands of memories with your loved one, many of which are bound to be humorous. So talk about that; talk about the amusing stories you have about your loved one, or tell someone about the funny stories your loved one used to tell you. You could also go out with a friend of yours that always makes you laugh, or you could watch a comedy movie, show, or online video—anything that makes you laugh, or at the very least, smile.

If you just can't laugh yet or you don't feel like you're ready to, that's perfectly fine. In time, you'll be able to breathe a little easier and begin to see the humor in things again, then you can laugh to your heart's content.

Accepting That You'll Always Carry Them with You

Whatever it is that you've lost—whether it be a loved one to death, a relationship to divorce, a dream to reality, or anything in between—it will stay with you forever, in some way or another. That doesn't mean that you'll be in pain forever, it just means that you will carry around a bit of that loss somewhere inside you, likely for the rest of your life. You may not even know it's there on most days, but it's a part of you now.

I've said this before, but when you lose someone, your bond with them *changes*, it doesn't go away at all. So don't try to force yourself to forget them, because it's never going to happen. What you do need to do is accept that your relationship with them, while not ending, will never be the same.

As you accept this fact and begin building yourself up again and moving forward with your life, you can still keep your loved one close to you in your day to day life. Here are just a few ways you can do that:

Talk to Them

Talk inside your head or out loud and do it daily, weekly, or just wherever you miss them. If it helps you feel more connected, you could visit their final resting place and talk to them when you can.

Write Letters to Them

Similar to talking to them, writing letters could help you feel connected to your loved one. Many people choose to get rid of the letters after they've written it as a symbol of the letter having reached their loved one.

Talk About Them

Talking about someone is what keeps their memory alive, so if you're hanging out with a friend or sitting at home with your significant other and an interesting or funny memory pops into your head, tell them about it.

Keep Something of Theirs in Your Space

Photos are the most common memento, but it can be anything that belonged to the person or was important to them, like an ornament or their favorite shirt. Like I said, I still have my grandmother's plastic butterflies. Keeping these items close to you on a daily basis instead of inside a display case can make you feel even closer to the person.

Make Them a Part of Your Daily Rituals

Set an extra place at the dinner table for them, add their favorite song to your playlist, or wear either their jewelry or a piece of jewelry that you had made from their ashes. Try and incorporate something about them into your daily routine.

Take Care of Yourself

The only way you can give your loved one the attention and respect they deserve is by first taking care of yourself.

Rest assured that as long as you never forget them and as long as you keep talking about them, your loved one's memory will remain alive inside you forever.

Worksheet #8

A Letter To Your Loved One

Write a letter to the person you lost.

_____

_____

_____

_____

_____

_____

_____

_____

_____

_____

Special Bonus

Want This _Free_ Book?

Great Free **Unlimited Access** To This Book and All My Other Books By Joining Below!

Scan W/ Your Camera

Conclusion

I know there was a lot of information packed into this book, and I'm not going to make you memorize every single point that's been brought up (there are no tests, I promise). But I just hope that something in here resonated with you in some way. I hope that you understand what grief is a little better. I hope that reading through this gives you ideas of how you're going to create your own grief game plan and navigate your way down the bumpy, twisty, uneven road that is your own grief.

Whether you suffer from survivor's guilt, grief from going through a divorce, unresolved grief, or anything in between, I want you to remember these three things, above everything else:

- Everybody grieves differently

- Be kind to yourself

- Give yourself time to heal

If you keep that in mind (and maybe write in a journal now and then, seeing as how I am the number one fan of journaling), then I have faith that you'll get through the worst times and end up in a place where you can remember your loved ones fondly.

I would love to hear about any of your experiences with using this book, or even just about your story of grief. You can follow me on Instagram @cortezranieri and DM me your story if you wish to.

I hope you have a good night, and that you smile just a little more tomorrow.

References

Ackerman, C. (2018 April 25). *Grief Counseling: Therapy Techniques for Children and Hospice Care.* PositivePsychology.com.
https://positivepsychology.com/grief-counseling/

Bennett, T. (2019 May 3). *Humor can help you manage grief and cope with loss - Thriveworks.* Counseling and Life Coaching - Find a Counselor. https://thriveworks.com/blog/humor-can-help-you-manage-grief-and-cope-with-loss/

Briana. (2020 May 12). *How To Practice Spiritual Self-Care To Soothe Your Soul.* Learning to Be Free. http://www.learningtobefree.com/2020/05/12/spiritual-self-care/

Burgess, J. (2019 December 16). *Simple ways to practise emotional self-care and transform your life.* Life Sorted. https://www.lifesorted.com/emotional-self-care/#:~:text=Emotional%20self%2Dcare%20can%20be

Centore, A. (n.d.). *How to Forgive Yourself — Letting Go of Past Regrets.* Https://Thriveworks.com/. https://thriveworks.com/blog/how-to-forgive-yourself/

Coping With Feelings Of Relief During Bereavement - Funeral Guide (n.d.). Www.funeralguide.co.uk. Retrieved February 1, 2022, from https://www.funeralguide.co.uk/help-resources/bereavement-support/coping-with-bereavement/coping-with-feelings-of-relief-during-bereavement

Coping with Grief, Tips for Handling Grief One Day at a Time (n.d.). GriefAndSympathy.com. Retrieved February 1, 2022, from https://www.griefandsympathy.com/copingwithgrief.html

Coping with Loss: Remembering a Loved One (n.d.). Let Your Love Grow. Retrieved February 1, 2022, from https://letyourlovegrow.com/blogs/blog/coping-with-loss-remembering-a-loved-one

Coping with relationship breakdown (2021). Betterrelationships.org.au. https://www.betterrelationships.org.au/relationships/coping-relationship-breakdown/

Dealing With Guilt After a Loss | Kaiser Permanente (n.d.). Healthy.kaiserpermanente.org. Retrieved February 1, 2022, from https://healthy.kaiserpermanente.org/health-wellness/health-encyclopedia/he.dealing-with-guilt-after-a-loss.aa128972

Definition of GRIEVE (n.d.). Www.merriam-Webster.com. Retrieved February 1, 2022, from https://www.merriam-webster.com/dictionary/grieve

familydoctor.org editorial staff. (2017, August 16). *Grieving: Facing Illness, Death, and Other Losses - familydoctor.org.* Familydoctor.org. https://familydoctor.org/grieving-facing-illness-death-and-other-losses/

8 Touching Ways to Keep a Loved One's Memory Alive (2021, October 21). Fatherly. https://www.fatherly.com/love-money/keep-a-loved-ones-memory-alive/

18 Personal Items to Keep After a Loved One Dies | Cake Blog (n.d.). Www.joincake.com. Retrieved February 1, 2022, from https://www.joincake.com/blog/what-to-keep-after-someone-dies/

11 Journaling Tips For People Who Are Absolutely TERRIBLE At Keeping A Journal (2018 December 19). Bustle. https://www.bustle.com/p/11-journaling-tips-for-people-who-are-absolutely-terrible-at-keeping-a-journal-15514789

11 Ways to Practice Emotional Self Care (n.d.). Choosing Therapy. Retrieved February 1, 2022, from https://www.choosingtherapy.com/emotional-self-care/

Feeling Stuck in Your Grief After a Death? 10 Tips to Help | Cake Blog. (n.d.). Www.joincake.com. Retrieved February 1, 2022, from https://www.joincake.com/blog/stuck-in-grief/

5 Benefits of Grief Journaling (2019 August 16). Whats Your Grief. https://whatsyourgrief.com/5-benefits-of-grief-journaling/

5 Self-Care Tips to Help Lessen Grief | Pathways Home Health (n.d.). Pathways Home Health and Hospice. Retrieved February 1, 2022, from https://pathwayshealth.org/grief-support/5-self-care-tips-to-help-lessen-grief/

Grief and Bereavement (n.d.). Www.cancer.org. Retrieved February 1, 2022, from https://amp.cancer.org/treatment/end-of-life-care/grief-and-loss/grieving-process.html

Grief Meaning | Best 9 Definitions of Grief (n.d.). Www.yourdictionary.com. Retrieved February 1, 2022, from https://www.yourdictionary.com/grief

Grief One Day at a Time: 365 Meditations to Help You Heal After Loss (n.d.). Center for Loss & Life Transition. Retrieved February 1, 2022, from https://www.centerforloss.com/bookstore/grief-one-day-time-365-meditations-help-heal-loss/

Grief vs. Mourning (2019 July 8). The Recovery Village Drug and Alcohol Rehab. https://www.therecoveryvillage.com/mental-health/grief/related/grief-vs-mourning/

Grief, W. Y. (2014 March 24). *16 Tips for Continuing Bonds with People We've Lost.* What's Your Grief. https://whatsyourgrief.com/16-practical-tips-continuing-bonds/

Grief, W. Y. (2014 June 18). *Photos of Deceased Loved Ones: The Great Debate.* What's Your Grief. https://whatsyourgrief.com/photos-of-deceased/

Grief, W. Y. (2014 December 11). *The Utility of Laughter in Times of Grief.* What's Your Grief. https://whatsyourgrief.com/laughter-in-times-of-grief/

Grief, W. Y. (2016 May 31). *Relief After A Death: The Unspoken Grief Emotion.* What's Your Grief. https://whatsyourgrief.com/relief-after-a-death-the-unspoken-emotion/

Grieving Someone You Didn't Know (or Hardly Knew) (2019 June 19). Whats Your Grief. https://whatsyourgrief.com/grieving-someone-you-didnt-know-or-hardly-knew/

Grieving Someone You Didn't Like (Because It Happens!) (2017 February 2). Whats Your Grief. https://whatsyourgrief.com/grieving-someone-you-didnt-like/

Guilt and Regret - Transitions LifeCare Bereavement Blog. (2020, January 29). Transitions LifeCare. https://www.transitionslifecare.org/2020/01/29/guilt-and-regret/

helpguidewp. (2019 January 7). *HelpGuide.org.* HelpGuide.org. https://www.helpguide.org/articles/grief/coping-with-grief-and-loss.htm

How To Choose The Right Bereavement Group | BetterHelp (n.d.). Www.betterhelp.com. https://www.betterhelp.com/advice/grief/how-to-choose-the-right-bereavement-group/

How to Cope When it Seems Like Everyone Wants to Forget (2019 January 30). Whats Your Grief. https://whatsyourgrief.com/ways-to-keep-your-loved-ones-memory-alive/

How to ease the pain of separation | Divorce | The Guardian (n.d.). Amp.theguardian.com. Retrieved February 1, 2022, from https://amp.theguardian.com/lifeandstyle/2011/feb/09/ease-pain-of-separation

How to Help Someone Who is Grieving | Cancer (n.d.). CancerCare. https://www.cancercare.org/publications/67-how_to_help_someone_who_is_grieving

How to journal about grief I Simple prompts to use (n.d.). Peacefully. https://guide.peacefully.com/resources/how-to-journal-about-grief

How to Manage Grief Through Journaling (n.d.). Www.brainandlife.org. https://www.brainandlife.org/the-magazine/online-exclusives/how-to-manage-grief-through-journaling/

How to process grief and find healthy ways to overcome loss (n.d.). Www.betterup.com. Retrieved February 1, 2022, from https://www.betterup.com/blog/how-to-process-grief?hs_amp=true

How to Start (and Keep) a DIY Grief Journal: Step-By-Step | Cake Blog (n.d.). Www.joincake.com. Retrieved

February 1, 2022, from https://www.joincake.com/blog/grief-journal/

https://www.facebook.com/verywell (2019). *Tips for Managing Survivor's Guilt.* Verywell Mind. https://www.verywellmind.com/survivors-guilt-4688743

Inhibited Grief: 10 Things to Know About Unresolved Grief» Urns | Online (n.d.). Www.usurnsonline.com. Retrieved February 1, 2022, from https://www.usurnsonline.com/grief-loss/inhibited-grief/

Is A Grief Support Group Right For You? (2021, November 22). Mindfulness & Grief: Meditation for Life after Loss. https://mindfulnessandgrief.com/is-a-grief-support-group-right-for-you/

Is it normal to feel guilty after someone dies? (2020, July 23). Help 2 Make Sense. https://help2makesense.org/is-it-normal-to-feel-guilty-after-someone-dies/

It's OK to Mourn the People You've Had to Cut Off (n.d.). Www.yahoo.com. Retrieved February 1, 2022, from https://www.yahoo.com/amphtml/lifestyle/ok-mourn-people-youve-had-154234669.html

Jane. (2015). *22 Ways to Practice Emotional Self-Care and Letting Go.* Habitsforwellbeing.com. https://www.habitsforwellbeing.com/22-ways-practice-emotional-self-care-letting-go/

Journaling for Healing (2021 June 22). Fullcirclegc.org. https://fullcirclegc.org/2021/06/22/journaling-for-healing/

Journaling Your Way Through Grief | Pathways. (n.d.). Pathways Home Health and Hospice. Retrieved February 1, 2022, from https://pathwayshealth.org/grief-support/journaling-your-way-through-grief/#:~:text=It

Klaric, M. (2020, September 19). *Take It One Day at a Time — Tips for Coping With Loss #2.* Transform the Pain. https://medium.com/transform-the-pain/take-it-one-day-at-a-time-tips-for-coping-with-grief-2-c2f42b523175#:~:text=To%20avoid%20getting%20stranded%20on

Losing a Best Friend: 7 Ways to Cope (2020 November 17). Healthline. https://www.healthline.com/health/losing-a-best-friend

Loss, Grief and Bereavement Treatment, Phases and Mourning on MedicineNet.com (n.d.). MedicineNet. https://www.medicinenet.com/script/main/art.asp?articlekey=83860

M.A, G. A., Marriage, & Therapy, F. (n.d.). *Grief vs. Mourning: Understanding the Differences.* LoveToKnow. Retrieved February 1, 2022, from https://dying.lovetoknow.com/ideas-advice-coping-grief/grief-vs-mourning-understanding-differences

Mayo Clinic. (2016). *What is grief?* Mayo Clinic. https://www.mayoclinic.org/patient-visitor-guide/support-groups/what-is-grief

Mayo Clinic Staff. (2017). *Complicated grief - Symptoms and causes.* Mayo Clinic. https://www.mayoclinic.org/diseases-conditions/complicated-grief/symptoms-causes/syc-20360374

Melinda. (2018 November 2). *Dealing with a Breakup or Divorce - HelpGuide.org.* Https://Www.helpguide.org. https://www.helpguide.org/articles/grief/dealing-with-a-breakup-or-divorce.htm

Memorialize Your Loved One In a Less-Than-Traditional Way (2019 July 1). Sonida Senior Living. https://www.sonidaseniorliving.com/memorialize-your-loved-one-in-a-less-than-traditional-way/

9 Self-Care Tips For Grief: Reduce Your Suffering in Mind, Body & Spirit (2017 January 20). Mindfulness & Grief: Meditation for Life after Loss. https://mindfulnessandgrief.com/9-self-care-tips-for-grief/

9 Ways to Honor a Loved One Who Has Passed (n.d.). CaringBridge. Retrieved February 1, 2022, from https://www.caringbridge.org/resources/9-ways-remember-loved-one-passed/

Paying Tribute: 10 Ways to Memorialize Your Loved Ones to Keep Their Memory Alive (2021 July 21). Eterneva - Remarkable Memorial Diamonds.

https://eterneva.com/blog/memorialize-loved-ones/

Quotes for Coping with the Loss of a Loved One (2019). Let Your Love Grow. https://letyourlovegrow.com/blogs/blog/quotes-for-coping-with-the-loss-of-a-loved-one

Relieving the heavy burden of survivor guilt (2019, June 27). Counseling Today. https://ct.counseling.org/2019/06/relieving-the-heavy-burden-of-survivor-guilt/

A Roadmap Through Grief: Finding Your Way After the Death of a Loved One (2019 March 25). The Healing Collective. https://www.healingcollective.ca/general/a-roadmap-through-grief-finding-your-way-after-the-death-of-a-loved-one/

Schneiderman, M. (2021 February 5). *It's Normal to Grieve After Divorce. These 16 Tips Can Help You Through It.* Fatherly. https://www.fatherly.com/love-money/divorce-grief-tips/amp/

Self-Care During Grief Tips: How to Create a Practical Self-Care Plan (2021, July 21). Eterneva - Remarkable Memorial Diamonds. https://eterneva.com/blog/self-care-during-grief-tips/

Self-Care While Grieving | Essentia Health (n.d.). Www.essentiahealth.org. https://www.essentiahealth.org/services/behavior

al-mental-health-services/grief-bereavement-support/resources/self-care-while-grieving/

64 Self-Care Ideas for Grievers (2014 February 25). Whats Your Grief. https://whatsyourgrief.com/self-care-ideas-for-grievers/

Sometimes We All Need An Escape, And That's Okay (2017 June 21). Thought Catalog. https://thoughtcatalog.com/david-dean/2017/06/sometimes-we-all-need-an-escape-and-thats-okay/

The Spiritual Side of Yoga — What it Means and How to Achieve it (n.d.). Himalayan Yoga Institute. https://www.himalayanyogainstitute.com/spiritual-side-yoga-means-achieve/

Stern, J., & LISW. (n.d.). *To Get Unstuck.* Transformative Grief. Retrieved February 1, 2022, from https://transformativegrief.com/2017/07/25/getting-unstuck/

Stuck in Grief? What to do when you can't move on (n.d.). Theskillcollective.com. Retrieved February 1, 2022, from https://theskillcollective.com/blog/stuck-in-grief?format=amp

Survivor Guilt (2016 September 8). GoodTherapy.org Therapy Blog. https://www.goodtherapy.org/blog/psychpedia/survivor-guilt

Team YourDOST. (2021 May 29). *Navigating Through Grief: Is There a Roadmap?* YourDOST Blog. https://yourdost.com/blog/2021/05/grief-counseling.html

10 Spiritual Self-Care Tips To Be Happy (2019 March 28). Chopra. https://chopra.com/articles/10-spiritual-self-care-tips-to-be-happy

The 10 Best Online Grief Support Groups of 2021 (2021 June 14). Healthline. https://www.healthline.com/health/mental-health/online-grief-support-groups

3 Reasons Why Memorialization Is Important to the Grieving Process (n.d.). Www.milanomonuments.com. Retrieved February 1, 2022, from https://www.milanomonuments.com/blog/3-reasons-why-memorialization-is-important-to-the-grieving-process?hs_amp=true

13 ways to keep a lost loved one's memory alive (2022). Gwic.com. https://www.gwic.com/Education-Center/Grief-Support/13-ways-to-keep-a-lost-loved-one%E2%80%99s-memory-alive

Top 5 Common Myths of Grief (n.d.). Hospice of the Red River Valley. Retrieved February 1, 2022, from https://www.hrrv.org/blog/top-5-common-myths-of-grief/

Top 10 Ways to Escape Reality and Relax (n.d.). Lifehacker.com. Retrieved February 1, 2022, from https://lifehacker.com/top-10-ways-to-escape-reality-and-relax-1792238208/amp

Twelve Myths about Grief - Cabell Huntington Hospital (n.d.). Cabellhuntington.org. Retrieved February 1, 2022, from https://cabellhuntington.org/services/counseling-services/twelve-myths-about-grief/

20 Ways to Take Care of Yourself While Grieving - Altru Blog (n.d.). Altru Health System. Retrieved February 1, 2022, from https://www.altru.org/blog/2019/august/20-ways-to-take-care-of-yourself-while-grieving/

Unique Ideas for Honoring the Memory of a Loved One (n.d.). Memorial Planning. Retrieved February 1, 2022, from https://www.memorialplanning.com/blog/15-unique-ideas-for-honoring-the-memory-of-a-loved-one

Unresolved Grief | Michigan Medicine (n.d.). Www.uofmhealth.org. https://www.uofmhealth.org/health-library/aa129324

What They Left Behind: Photos of Things People Kept to Remember Their Deceased Loved Ones - VICE (n.d.). Www.vice.com. Retrieved February 1, 2022, from https://www.vice.com/amp/en/article/jm593p/what-they-left-behind-photos-of-things-people-kept-to-remember-their-deceased-loved-ones

What to Do When You Don't Feel Like Journaling Ever Again (n.d.). Www.createwritenow.com. Retrieved February 1, 2022, from https://www.createwritenow.com/journal-writing-blog/bid/86591/What-to-Do-When-You-Don-t-Feel-Like-Journaling-Ever-Again?hs_amp=true

What's a Grief Retreat? And How Do They Work? | Cake Blog (n.d.). Www.joincake.com. Retrieved February 1, 2022, from https://www.joincake.com/blog/grief-retreat/

What's Your Grief (2015 August 4). *64 Myths About Grief That Just Need To STOP.* What's Your Grief. https://whatsyourgrief.com/64-myths-about-grief-that-just-need-to-stop/

What's Your Grief. (2016 August 2). *The Unique Loneliness of Grief.* What's Your Grief. https://whatsyourgrief.com/unique-loneliness-grief/

What's Your Grief. (2017 April 12). *Guilt and Grief: coping with the shoulda, woulda, couldas.* What's Your Grief. https://whatsyourgrief.com/guilt-and-grief-2/

Printed in Great Britain
by Amazon

27596136R00101